BREAD, BUTTER, AND SUGAR

A Boy's Journey Through the Holocaust and Postwar Europe

Martin Schiller

Hamilton Books

A member of

ROWMAN & LITTLEFIELD PUBLISHERS, INC.

Lanham • Boulder • New York • Toronto • Plymouth, UK

Copyright © 2007 by
Hamilton Books
4501 Forbes Boulevard
Suite 200
Lanham, Maryland 20706
Hamilton Books Acquisitions Department (301) 459-3366

Estover Road
Plymouth PL6 7PY
United Kingdom

Library of Congress Control Number: 2006935859
ISBN-13: 978-0-7618-3571-4 (paperback : alk. paper)
ISBN-10: 0-7618-3571-7 (paperback : alk. paper)

I dedicate this autobiography to my father Marcus Schiller
and all the members in my family who perished
at the hands of the Nazis and
whose markers were never to be.

May this book serve to honor their memory and
celebrate their existence as loving, caring and gentle human beings.

Contents

Preface

For many years after WW II, I felt an unrelenting emptiness in my heart because I had no graves or visible markers to visit. On many occasions I needed to unload my innermost feelings and express my sense of loss. Yet there were no graves, no tombstones, and no markers.

This autobiography is the fulfillment of an obligation to the many victims in the Holocaust who at one time or another touched my life. It is a self-imposed obligation to transmit a document in the name of those whose voices were forever stilled before their time by their Nazi tormentors. I witnessed their cries. I witnessed the depth of their agony. This book is in part my "Kaddish" for them, when I no longer am able to stand up on their behalf.

I have tried to report, as best as my memory serves me, an account of events as I lived them and saw them with my own eyes. These early childhood-robbing events shaped my vision of life, my very nature, and my soul. I have chosen to tell my story in the third person in order to describe my thoughts and emotions as a child who experienced these events. For several years now, I have given talks to high school students about my experiences during the Holocaust. I was moved by their ability to relate to my experiences and encouraged by their capacity for caring about other human beings. Maybe the next generation can learn from this sad history.

I am now seventy-three years old. Having laid out my life on these pages, I fervently hope that the completion of this autobiography will serve to dislodge the albatross from around my neck. Tomorrow I may be here no more. Therefore, I hope that this book will help to blunt any revisionist attempts to stain the memories of the innocent souls that suffered at the Nazi hands.

Acknowledgments

I am grateful to my son Marc, who in spite of my initial refusal to return to Poland and Germany, persisted for a number of years in encouraging me to make this trip—to allow him the experience of walking on the very same ground that his father, grandfather and the many members of his "lost family" walked. He insisted on making this "heritage trip" with his father at his side. I finally agreed, out of pure love for my son. However, taking that trip with my family at my side, even though a terribly emotional experience, turned out to be an unexpectedly comforting catharsis for me.

A special thanks to my wife Elaine, who for forty-eight years has put up with all of my idiosyncrasies. She has been my lifelong "buddy" who consistently encouraged me in all my undertakings. I particularly want to thank her for her lifetime support and unending patience with me.

Special thanks also to Bonny V. Fetterman, an exceptional editor, whose professionalism surfaced instantly. She gently but firmly guided this book to publication.

Chapter One

An Abbreviated Childhood

It was a hot August afternoon in Tarnobrzeg, Poland. The sun was starting its descent into the western horizon behind the evergreen trees. Playful children's voices filled the air throughout the courtyard. A gentle, warm breeze carried Menush's voice to his mother's ears.

Menush's mother took delight in watching her six-year-old son marching like a soldier, shouting military orders to the neighborhood children, most of them older than her son. He was already leading their games with an authority that demanded respect from the other children. His Bubby was also drawn to the window. She and Zaidy lived with them ever since Zaidy became ill.

Bubby rested her arm on her daughter's shoulder as she too delighted in the scene that was unfolding outside in the courtyard. From their kitchen window, Menush's mother and grandmother had a panoramic view of the whole courtyard, including the entranceway that led from the street.

The courtyard was set back several hundred feet from a relatively busy avenue named Mitczkewice Uliza. The main entrance had large swing gates. The gates were always wide open. The rear exit gates, located to the left rear of Menush's house, were smaller. They led to the forest and the river. Obliquely to the left of the house was the water well and beyond that was Shaya's house. He was known as "Shaya the Cobbler." He and his wife lived in a three-bedroom house with their ten children, ranging in age from two to thirteen. Shaya had his shop in the house. He catered primarily to the upper crust, providing them with handmade shoes and boots to order.

Menush enjoyed playing with Shaya's children. They always seemed to be available whenever he was out in the courtyard, very likely because it was so crowded in their house. On occasion when Menush was inside Shaya's house during mealtime, his wife would invite him to eat too. He loved sitting at the long, wobbly wooden table covered with a stained tablecloth and taking in the aroma of a freshly cooked potato soup mixed with the fragrance of new shoe leather. As a reciprocating gesture, Menush's mother frequently invited all of Shaya's children for supper. But he preferred eating in the cobbler's house — except for when Bubby made his special white borsht.

During the warm spring days, Bubby cooked his favorite meal especially for him: white borsht (*schav*), a creamy spinach soup. She would wait for him at the door with her lovingly warm smile when he came home from kindergarten, holding a small pot in her hands.

For a while this was an almost daily ritual. As he ran up to the door, she hugged and kissed him. Then she sat him down in his little chair and served him his white borsht. She sat next to him, aglow with grandmotherly pleasure, as he scooped up every last spoonful. Then Menush would wipe the inside of the little pot clean with a slice of freshly baked bread. Family members and neighbors were never sure which of the two enjoyed this ritual more.

The courtyard was an oasis-like environment. It was removed from the hustle and bustle of the city streets. If you stepped out onto the avenue and turned to the right, the road led you to the city hospital and to Uncle Ephraim's store. If you turned to the left, it led you to the synagogue and to the city center. The courtyard was surrounded by single-family homes arranged almost in a full circle. In the center was a large circular garden filled with a wide array of colorful plants and flowers. The most eye-catching attraction was the tall sunflower arrangement carefully placed in a circle so that no matter where you stood, you could appreciate their full beauty.

A favorite summertime activity for the children was to ride their bicycles around this circular garden. It was a time when the plants and flowers were in full bloom. The melodic chirping of birds blended seamlessly with the chatter of playful children. Young mothers engaged in casual conversation while rocking their infants. The aroma of fresh baked bread wafted out onto the courtyard intermingling with the fragrance of the flowers.

There was an unwritten law that each child knew instinctively: Never to enter the garden proper. Menush enjoyed riding his father's bicycle around the periphery of the garden. He was too small to straddle the crossbar, so he placed his right foot and body under the bar and pedaled the bicycle clockwise around the garden in this position.

The neighbors were quite amused by this scene. His Bubby, however, was not. She was very nervous about it and made no secret of it. She repeatedly chided her daughter for allowing her little boy to ride the bicycle in such a precarious manner. But Menush's mother took pleasure in watching her adventurous son, beaming with joy whenever he had the opportunity to ride his tall father's "grown-up" bicycle. He frequently looked back in his mother's direction to make sure that she was watching. He loved his mother and having her approval meant a great deal to him.

Menush's father worked late hours, even after he came home. During the week, Menush was cared for by his mother and grandmother, but on Saturdays he would have his father's full attention. His father was his hero. The few times that his mother made him stand in the corner for misbehaving, he found comfort in looking forward to Saturday when he could unload his troubles to his father.

Saturdays in the summertime were especially enjoyable. These were the days when the three "men"—Menush, his father, and older brother Chamush—walked to synagogue together, with Menush on one side of their father and Chamush on the other. Sometimes they were even allowed to go to services with their father on Friday evening.

A special bonus for Menush was to hear the voice of Reb Sholom lead the congregation in prayer. Reb Sholom was a neighbor who lived with his wife and children only two houses down the courtyard, to the right of Menush's house. He was a tall, thin man with a slightly reddish beard and carried himself with an erect stature.

Reb Sholom had a very haunting tenor voice. Menush loved to listen to him, especially when he led the congregation in prayer on the High Holidays. His voluminous rich voice filled every crevice of the synagogue walls. When he sang out, "Hear our voices, Lord our God . . .," Menush trembled along with the walls. His melodic chants crept into Menush's veins and surged their way through his soul, to remain forever locked up in his heart.

His tones, his fervent pleas molded into opera like phrases, creating an atmosphere of awe and pleasure. One didn't have to be an adult to be swept along by his melodious prayers. Reb Sholom's voice transported the whole congregation to a magical place where every participant felt connected to all of Israel, standing in the presence of those that came before.

An additional Saturday afternoon treat for Menush, during the long summer days, was to accompany his father to a place called the *"shenk."* This was the time when he had his father exclusively to himself, because his brother did not care to take part in this adventure.

The *shenk* was a beer hall that was closed on Saturdays to the public. Every Saturday afternoon it became a private club, visited primarily by modern Orthodox men. Chickpeas and beer were the only items on the menu and they were served on an honor system. Since no one spent money on the Sabbath the bills were paid afterwards. Menush felt like a grown-up when his father allowed him to take a few sips of beer along with his own, separate serving of chickpeas. Chess, Talmudic discussions, political debates, and good camaraderie, were of course, free of charge.

Menush particularly enjoyed watching his father play chess. When his father smelled victory, he would look at his son and give him a familiar wink that said, "I've got him." He usually greeted victory with a soft smile and a humble "thank you" to his opponent. The party always ended abruptly thirty minutes before the men had to depart for afternoon prayers.

The happy conclusion to the Sabbath day came when Uncle Ephraim came to visit Bubby, his sister. Menush had a special affection for Uncle Ephraim, who was a Talmud scholar with a good secular education as well. He owned a general store in town that carried both domestic and imported goods. Menush loved visiting his store. It was located on the major thoroughfare, halfway between the courtyard and the hospital. His uncle generally greeted him with a big hello and a piece of candy. Menush felt like an explorer when he walked around the store amid the goods from all over the world. Just touching the various sacks made him feel as if he had visited far-off lands. Uncle Ephraim was a man in his early fifties with a successful merchant's stomach, a small graying beard, sparkling eyes, and an infectious smile. When he walked into the house, the lights seemed to shine a little brighter and the conversation always became more animated.

He always came with two shiny new zlotys in his pocket to play a game with Menush and his brother. Uncle Ephraim would withdraw a coin from his pocket and offer it to Menush or to Chamush. When they reached for the coin, it would disappear into his sleeve. This game went on for several minutes until Zaidy said, "Enough, don't tease the children any longer." By that point, the children managed to snatch the coin from his hand as Uncle Ephraim laughed with delight. Menush enjoyed this game, knowing full well that eventually he would get his sparkling coin. It was a perfect end to a perfect day.

The children's happy clamor in the courtyard brought a welcome relief to their parents on an otherwise troubling day in August of 1939. The news that morning had created a somber mood in the city's Jewish community. A genuinely warm smile was nowhere to be found. Menush knew that something was wrong because neither his parents nor his grandparents came to his bedside that night to deliver his snack of buttered bread sprinkled on top with sugar.

Buttered bread sprinkled with sugar was a well-known ritual in Menush's family. A year earlier, he had been ill with pneumonia. His high fever lingered for a long time. He lost his appetite and was unable to eat for several days. This, of course, raised a great deal of concern in the family.

When the fever finally broke late one night, he woke up and asked for food. His Bubby had been sitting in a chair beside his bed, maintaining an all-night vigil. When she heard her grandson speak, she cried tears of joy and said, "You can have anything you want."

"Can I have bread and butter with sugar sprinkled on top?" he asked.

Within minutes his parents and grandparents paraded into his room with a tray full of buttered bread slices and sugar sprinkled on top with a tall glass of milk, but he soon fell asleep again before he could finish one slice.

The following night he woke up and asked for the same snack. And so started the ritual of the bread, butter and sugar every night between eleven and midnight. Most of the time he ate his snack with eyes closed, to the delight of his mother.

On this night, however, Menush was awakened by the sounds of the radio in the living room. It was unusually loud. There was no midnight snack at his bedside. He sensed that something was not quite right.

He rose from his bed and quietly walked over to the door, opening it just wide enough to peek out into the living room. He was surprised to see the whole family, still fully dressed, hovering around the radio. The mood was very somber and there was tension in the air. Menush did not ask for, nor did he feel like having his midnight snack any longer.

He stood at the door now fully awake trying to understand what the grown-ups were saying. They were speaking of things completely foreign to him, yet he sensed a tension that frightened him in a way that he never felt before. He recognized it was very late for everyone to be up, especially for Bubby and Zaidy. Menush also knew it was not a usual time for Uncle Ephraim or Reb Sholom to be visiting.

Uncle Ephraim normally came on Saturday nights, rarely at any other time. His voice was generally a melodious, gentle basso. This time it was deliberately muted and hardly audible. Reb Sholom's voice too was unnaturally hushed and filled with anguish.

Periodically, Menush heard the word "Hitler" creep into the conversation. He too began to feel an unnatural tension that was palpable in every corner of the house. This was the night when Menush learned three new words, words that would be engrained in his mind forever: "Blitzkrieg," "War," and "Hitler." From the hushed conversations and the tension that seemed to envelope those words, he instinctively associated those terms with fear.

The tension penetrated Menush's whole being. He realized it was not a good time to be asking for his snack, even if he had still wanted it. And so he went back to bed, laid his head on the pillow, and continued to listen until he fell asleep. His sleep was full of dreams of earlier, more pleasant days.

Tarnobrzeg in 1939 was a small industrial city located in the southeast corner of Poland, on the east bank of the Visla River. The total population was approximately six thousand. Sixty percent of the population was made up of Jewish families.

The news that war was coming to Poland, and the particular threat it posed to the Jews, was an ominous cloud that hung over the city. Those who had the means and the connections had either left already or were in the process of leaving the city, and ultimately Poland. In the late summer of 1939, the escape exits were pretty much closed to Menush and his family.

Chapter Two

The Rapid Ascent to Adulthood

A few weeks later terror struck the city. Menush never saw such raw fear in the eyes of his parents. Bombs were falling everywhere. The screams of people running in all directions, the earsplitting whistles of the bombs cutting through the air, the howls of the air raid sirens, the incessant clanging of the fire brigade vehicles, all struck such fear in Menush's heart that he began to shake uncontrollably. His parents gathered some clothes and immediate essentials and hurried with the two children in tow towards the river. Bubby insisted on remaining in the house, expecting the bombardment soon to stop. Menush and Chamush held on tightly to each other's hand as they fled with their parents. The thunder of the exploding bombs drove everyone from the burning inferno. At the riverbank, they and several other families hired a boat to ferry them across the river, away from the bombardment and the resulting firestorm.

Sitting in the boat, Menush calmed down a little. He looked back at the city skyline, observing the huge fires and the red sky over the city. He still needed to be assured by his parents that the fire would not reach them and engulf the small boat. Menush asked a thousand questions—why, who and why again: "Why is the sky so red? Why are they throwing bombs? Who are the Germans? Why don't they like us? When can we go back home? Where are we going?" His father, having been quiet throughout the whole trip, finally blurted out "Be quiet and don't ask so many questions!" Menush fell silent and cried quietly in his mother's trembling arms. Chamush cried too, as did most of the passengers in the crowded boat.

The Visla River was a familiar place to Menush. In the summertime it was a wonderful place for swimming and cavorting with his brother in its cool waters. In the wintertime it was their favorite place for ice-skating and sledding.

Yet the thought of crossing this wide river in such a small boat instilled in him a new fear. To Menush, the other side of the river was a faraway world. Without prior warning or mental preparation, he suddenly realized that they were approaching an unknown shore. He was seized by mixed emotions—fear of the unknown mingled with a sense of adventure, a pioneering feeling that soon overshadowed the terror he felt earlier. Soon he could see the landing site was only several hundred yards away. The shore was illuminated by the light of the fires burning in Tarnobrzeg on the other side of the river.

Koprzywnica, unlike Tarnobrzeg, was a very small town that had no industry and therefore held no strategic value. Located on the west side of the Visla, its existence on the map could be easily overlooked and its Jewish population was small. There the family rented a two-bedroom house as a temporary escape haven. It was close enough for a one-day commute by foot or horse and buggy to Tarnobrzeg, only a few kilometers away. Menush's father gradually transferred most of the family possessions from Tarnobrzeg to Koprzywnica. Bubby chose to stay in Tarnobrzeg, as did most of the family members and friends. Zaidy had passed away several weeks before the German onslaught. He got his wish—"not to be around when Hitler came to visit."

At first the commute was pretty routine and uneventful, but as weeks turned into months, travel for Jews became risky as harassments and murders by Germans as well as Poles were reported more frequently. This forced his father to travel mostly at night, off the roads and through the forest, in order to avoid detection. He and a Polish Gentile had a financial arrangement in a small manufacturing shop that produced residential wall insulation. However, after the German occupation of Tarnobrzeg, freedom of movement for Jews in particular became extremely difficult. And so the family became increasingly reliant on the moral and ethical sensibilities of their Polish business partner. He eventually proved to be unworthy of trust, selling off the company's assets while claiming losses.

Early one morning, Menush's father returned from an overnight trip. His whole body was shaking, his trousers were torn, and his coat was missing. He reached for his children, held them very tightly and cried uncontrollably. He kept repeating, "You have a newborn father. You have newborn father." The uncomprehending children and their mother joined him in tearful sobbing until he was able to speak. When he finally regained his composure, he described how a German soldier stopped him in the forest and was about to shoot him, but the soldier became distracted by some gunfire. At that point, he made a split second decision to run off, with the soldier shooting after him. Later that afternoon, he embraced his wife and said quietly to her in Yiddish, "Our parents are no longer here." She let out a heart-wrenching scream, deliberately tore the lapel of her blouse, and dropped like a rock to the floor.

Menush had never seen his parents in such a state. All composure was drained out of them. He once again felt a mixture of fear and panic. His parents, the very emotional lynchpins that he had become so dependent upon, were weakening all around him. Yiddish was Menush's first language, therefore he understood his father's words but he could not immediately grasp their meaning. His instincts made him afraid to ask, fearing the worst. He also sensed that the answers from his parents would be short and curt.

Since the night of the bombardment, Menush was asking less frequently the multitude of questions that normally well up in a child's mind. An increasing loss of innocence contributed to this process. And so started the gradual practice of suppressing questions. Menush began accepting things as they were, learning to listen in the presence of adults and asking very few questions. Restless sleeping became the norm for Menush. He made no requests for bread, butter and sugar as food became scarcer.

Uncle Ephraim had an only child, Hanue, a daughter of about sixteen. When the *"Einsatzgruppen,"* the Nazi killing squads, were approaching Krakow and points east, her parents sent her to Koprzywnica to live with her cousin, Menush's mother. Several months after her arrival, Menush was listening to an adult conversation and overheard the stinging Yiddish words: "Uncle Ephraim and his wife are no longer here."

The news brought Menush to tears, followed by intense anger. He went outside and began throwing rocks at the outhouse located several hundred feet from the house. Hanue was only told of her parents' fate several months later. By then, she had become an integral member of Menush's family.

One morning a friend of the family came to deliver a package. Menush was sitting on the steps near the door when he heard the man say in a very halting Yiddish, "Shaya the Cobbler is no longer here."

When Menush's mother cried out, "What will happen to his wife and children?" her friend answered, "They are no longer here either."

Menush, who now understood what this meant, ran to the outhouse and frantically began throwing rocks at its walls. He was infuriated at not being able to destroy it.

Soon thereafter, word came that the *Einsatzgruppen* slaughtered all the Jews who did not escape from Tarnobrzeg. As the seasons passed, the outhouse became increasingly pockmarked with countless lesions, the scars of Menush's rage.

Life in Koprzywnica, however, took on a strange type of guarded normalcy, even though there were reports that Jews in most cities were being deported on trains to unknown destinations. Some families made preparations to hide on farms, in haylofts, in cellars, in attics. Such measures, if they were to succeed, required an abiding trust in their hosts and their neighbors. This avenue proved fatal for many Jews who were later betrayed. Still some lived in a state of denial, believing the worst was over and that better days lay ahead. In the face of this utter helplessness, denial was their means to prevent insanity.

In the early period of the German invasion, many people parroted the rumors that the war would be over in a matter of months. They called it a "Blitzkrieg," a flash in the pan. Therefore, the prevailing logic was that all one had to do was just to sit tight and wait it out. Of course, the religious Jews continued saying psalms and fasting. Some were even convinced that if times were so hard, the Messiah must surely be just around the corner.

When money and food supplies became scarce, Menush's mother began selling off her furs, jewelry, and fancy dresses. His father continued his dangerous trips to nearby cities, trading in a variety of goods for a little cash.

Uncle Avrohom, his father's brother, also came to town with his wife and two children— a teenaged girl named Chana and a ten-year-old boy, Chaim. Chana was a vivacious, warm, and loving young lady. Menush fell in love with her instantly. She always had a warm smile for the younger children. For Menush, her arrival was the perfect antidote to the gloom that prevailed in their home. Chana also adored her little brother and watched over him as if he were her son. Menush loved Chana, partly because she took such good care of her brother and partly because of her zest for life. She devised wonderful games for all the children and never lost her patience like the adults.

The children of the two respective families grew very close in a relatively short period of time. That summer, they enjoyed swimming together in a small stream that ran adjacent to the house. The stream dropped off into a waterfall and under a bridge that stood diagonally opposite from the house. The house, which stood on a gradual decline from the road, afforded an excellent view of the town's main artery. Menush liked to sit on the steps and watch the traffic from a safe distance.

The sight of a German soldier struck terror in all the adults. Yet one warm day in the fall, Menush stood in front of his house admiring German soldiers and their sharp uniforms as they rode by in an endless convoy of trucks and artillery vehicles. He found himself wishing that he could be one of them. He even dreamt about it that night. The following morning and several days thereafter he experienced terrible pangs of guilt for having favorable thoughts of Germans. He was supposed to hate them! He was afraid to share this with anyone lest he be considered a traitor. And so once again, he pelted the outhouse with rocks.

Menush desperately missed his friend Sahnek, a stray dog that he had befriended in Tarnobrzeg. He loved that little mutt. The dog weighed about thirty pounds. He had a short brown and white fur coat, a wet beagle nose, and wagged his tail like a metronome. The mutt was his best friend and confidant. Whenever his Bubby or Zaidy saw him holding the dog, and especially when the animal licked his face, they were horrified. It was not in their culture to either own or interact with domesticated animals. His parents were more accepting of his pet. He was allowed to feed and pet the dog, but he could not bring him into the house. On many occasions Sahnek was a source of comfort when Menush became angry with his parents or his brother. He knew that he could always talk to Sahnek. Now he found himself wishing that he could share his feelings with his best friend again.

In the early fall of 1942, the Jews approached the High Holy Days, the "Days of Awe," with heavy hearts. The air was heavy with a sense of despair and doom. Many Jews prayed in small groups in non-conspicuous homes. There was no singing, just heartwrenching cries for help. These were not the melodious prayers that Menush remembered from Reb Sholom. He wondered if indeed his grandparents and Uncle Ephraim were sitting in heaven, listening. Menush did not understand the words that were being uttered, yet he was swept up with the pleas ascending to heaven. He quietly prayed along with the rest of the congregation:

> From the depths I called You, God
> My Lord hear my voice,
> May Your ears be attentive to the sound of my pleas. . .

Menush's seventh and eighth birthdays had long passed without any notice. His ninth year was coming over the horizon and his only education to date consisted of kindergarten. He was jealous of his brother's ability to read, and particularly his ability to practice his reading with minimal help from the adults. Chamush could also do simple additions and subtractions. Menush's mother had neither the time nor the patience to teach him to read. She was struggling in a daily battle for the family's survival.

Menush became more interested in adult conversations than child's play. His ears perked up whenever anyone discussed current events, even though the news was generally very depressing. He once asked his mother, "Why does everyone want to kill the Jews? Why doesn't God help?" Her answer was, "When you grow up, you will understand."

But Menush needed to understand right now! He began suspecting that God was punishing them and tried to recall if his family had done anything wrong. He remembered an incident in Tarnobrzeg when his mother, in a fit of anger, threw a pan full of scrambled eggs on the floor. Chamush was considered a poor eater. One morning his mother had particular difficulty coaxing him to eat breakfast. He refused everything that she served. Finally he said he would eat scrambled eggs. As she was taking the eggs off the stove he said, "I don't want them."

Without a word she threw the eggs onto the floor and stormed out of the kitchen. Bubby came into the kitchen, cleaned the floor and chided her daughter, saying, "It is a sin to throw away food!" Those words came back to haunt Menush on a number of occasions, particularly when food became scarce.

Meanwhile, the vise on the Jewish communities kept closing ever tighter. Indiscriminate killing of Jews all over Poland became the norm rather then the exception. Concentration camps were constructed all over the eastern portion of the country. Those who were not caregivers to their immediate family members ran off to fight with the partisans or went into hiding. Parents with small children were running out of options. Of course, they continued to pray:

> Our brothers, the entire family of Israel,
> who are delivered into distress and captivity. . .
> May God have mercy on them and remove them from distress to relief,
> from darkness to light, from subjugation to redemption,
> Now, speedily and soon. . .

Late in November of 1942, word came from the *"Judenrat,"* the Jewish Council of Koprzywnica, that a round-up of all Jews was imminent. A round-up meant that Jews would be gathered to face the Nazi killing squads or be deported on trains to concentration camps.

Uncle Avrohom and his family fled the town. Menush's father paid a farmer to hide the family in the haystacks that stood in the field. The haystack option turned out to be a risky choice. Firstly, Chamush was a restless sleeper and talked out loud in his sleep, therefore detection was a high likelihood. Secondly, the haystack was very uncomfortable and cold, so any thoughts of a prolonged stay was out of the question. After the second night the farmer complained about noises coming from the haystacks in the middle of the night and demanded more money. Menush's parents were convinced that even if the farmer could be trusted, at the first sign of trouble, his wife or son would turn the family over to the Nazis. On the third night, the family returned to their house.

A few days later, Menush's father walked into the house and collapsed into a chair. His jacket had a deliberate tear at the collar and his eyes were bloodshot. Menush did not ask his father a single question; instead he hugged his "Tatush" and held on to him until "Momushu" came into the room. Then he told them that his brother, Uncle Avrohom, had returned to Tarnobrzeg with his family, thinking that the round-ups were over. He, his wife Gitel, and their two children, Chana and Chaim, "were no longer here."

Menush no longer ran into the yard to pelt the outhouse with stones. He had seen the deliberate tears in collars, a Jewish sign of mourning, too many times already to react with anything but utter numbness. Chana, his beautiful cousin, would not leave his consciousness for many weeks thereafter. Her radiant face kept returning to him in the stillness of the night.

Running in any direction was no longer possible. The Nazi snares, coupled with the willing participation of some Poles, created maddening feelings of helplessness. Travel and trading, having become extremely dangerous, came to a complete halt. Resources for food and shelter became scarce. Desperation ruled each day. Menush's two young parents in their middle thirties, in the prime of their lives, who only a few short years earlier prepared for a bright future, were now aging rapidly with the crushing responsibility of making life and death decisions for themselves and their children.

Hanue, a vivacious young woman with a beautiful operatic voice, who came from a happy, well-to-do home, gradually grew melancholy and silent. Before the war she had been a true image of her father, Uncle Ephraim—always cheerful, with an infectious laugh that affected everyone around her. Now she too despaired as she cast in her lot with Menush's parents.

Then, suddenly, an illusion of hope seemed to appear. Word came from the *Judenrat,* the Jewish Council, that the Germans were looking for able-bodied men and women to work in an ammunition factory in Skarzysko-Kamienna, approximately fifty kilometers northwest of Koprzywnica. A promise was given that shelter and ample food would be provided to those who were willing to work. Young families with children were invited, but only with children who were twelve years old or older. The key words that lessened the fear of a Gestapo trap were "able-bodied" and "no children under twelve,"— namely, people who were able to work. Menush's father had a friend in the *Judenrat* who was instrumental in drawing up papers documenting that nine-year-old Menush was twelve and his eleven-year-old brother Chamush was thirteen.

Word was passed that space on the transportation trucks was limited, therefore only bare essentials could be taken, one rucksack per person. There was little time given to prepare, less than twelve hours. Mother Nature also conspired against the reluctant travelers. She produced a brutally cold wind on that late November afternoon. The air was thick with tension, turmoil, and misgivings, infecting every Jewish soul in the town. People who signed up for the trip arrived and assembled as ordered at the marketplace. By evening, several trucks arrived in the town center and began loading passengers.

Those who were going were tormented with fear, ambivalence, and uncertainty. As they sat in the open transport trucks, they questioned and re-evaluated their decision, praying that they made the right choice. Those who stayed behind were also tortured by their decision, which very soon turned out to be fatal.

As Menush watched the scene, he recalled the fateful words from the Yom Kippur prayers:

. . . who shall live and who shall die,
who shall come to a timely end, and who to an untimely end;
who shall perish by fire and who by water,
who by hunger and who by thirst. . .

Chapter Three

Introduction to Hell

As the transport truck tailgates were opened, the German SS greeted the new arrivals to Skarzysko with screams of the foulest language, accompanied by blood- curdling barks and growls of saliva-dripping, vicious German shepherd dogs. Screams of *"Raus!!* (Out!)" *"Schnell!!* (Fast!)" *"Schwein-hund-Jude!* (Pig-Jew-dog!)" were followed by well-placed whiplashes on the head and body to anyone who did not move fast enough. Any man or woman who dared to look into the eyes of the tormenters was beaten to a pulp. And for good measure, if one of the dogs were let loose, they too would literally get a piece of the action. Menush never saw, nor was he ever told about, the existence of such two-legged and four-legged animals.

Within thirty minutes of their arrival his mother was torn from his side and shipped off to another camp. Before she boarded the truck she attempted to say something to her children, but was stopped by a full-fisted blow to her face. Menush watched his mother stumble to the ground with blood dripping from her mouth, still forcing a smile to her husband with a motion that implied she was fine. At the same instant Menush felt the iron grip of his father's hand, which said, "Don't move and don't cry." Menush turned from a child into an adult in a matter of seconds.

The "sh" at the end of the name Menush implies "my dear" or "my dearest." It is generally attached in Polish to names of little children. After their arrival in Skarzysko, the boys began using their birth certificate names, Henek and Menek. However, when the two brothers addressed each other in the privacy of their own company it was as "Chamush" and "Menu."

Skarzysko was a slave labor camp. It was created for the sole purpose of providing labor for the factories that were manufacturing ammunition for German troops on the Eastern front. The factory complex, with its associated slave labor camps, was subdivided into three divisions. These divisions were separated by several kilometers from each other. They were named *"Werk A," "Werk B,"* and *"Werk C."*

Werk A and *Werk B* were primarily sites where small weapons ammunition was manufactured. *Werk C,* the most notorious, was known for its production of mines. The Jews assigned to *Werk C* were for all practical purposes sentenced to a slow, agonizing death. The work there necessitated coming into intimate contact with picric acid.

Picric acid is an explosive compound used in mines. Exposure to it for any length of time without personal safety protection causes kidney and liver failure. The process begins with a yellowing of the skin, red blood cell destruction and severe eye irritation. Its symptoms also include an incessant cough, vomiting and diarrhea. The Jews sent to *Werk C* usually died within a year.

Menek stood motionless in the howling cold wind, too terrified to cry out, as he watched his mother and his cousin Hanue carted off in a truck to *Werk B.* His principal support pillar was suddenly and abruptly taken from him. He, his brother and father, along with several dozen males, were marched off to a barrack in *Werk A.*

No civilized human being, let alone a nine and an eleven-year-old boy, could have been properly prepared for the scenes that unfolded in the initial days of their arrival at the camp. Men and women were kept in separate barracks. Each barrack contained long rows of three-tiered wooden bunk shelves butted together on opposite walls. All bunk shelves were lined with urine-stained, lice-infested straw. Each shelf was supposed to sleep five people side by side.

Large wooden crates that were located on the outside of the barracks, several hundred feet apart, contained human cadavers. The stench of death from these boxes was revolting at first, but within a couple of weeks the smell disappeared from one's consciousness. Once or twice a week, depending on the fill up rate, a crew of prisoners came by with a flatbed pushcart to haul away the corpses. On occasion if "the clean-up crew" piled the corpses too high, one or two bodies would fall off during the transport. The haulers would then either heave the corpse back onto the pile, or throw it into the nearest box for the next pick-up.

Lay us down to sleep, Lord our God, in peace,
And spread over us the shelter of Your peace. . .

The ever-present threat of death for the slightest infraction hung like the sword of Damocles over everyone's head. The work rule was very simple: "If you meet your quota on the assembly line, you will receive your food ration. If you don't, you starve that day. If you miss too many times, your life is not cost-effective, therefore, your elimination will serve to make room for a more productive slave." Simple German SS logic.

Stomach-wrenching hunger became Menek's constant companion. Again and again the picture of his mother throwing the eggs on the floor came back to haunt him. Why did his grandmother have to say, "It is a sin to throw away food"? Could God be so severe for such a small infraction?

The Skarzysko camp served two meals per day. It consisted of a slice of bread with black coffee in the morning and twelve hours later, after the work shift, a ladleful of soup. Menek prayed that the *"Kapo"* doling out the soup would dip the ladle down to the bottom of the tub and thus retrieve the belly-filling stock.

Food began to take center stage in all his dreams. A recurrent dream was seeing his Bubby greet him once again at the door, with her warm adoring smile, holding a little pot of borsht. He so desperately wished that he could have just one single slice of bread, butter and sugar. Prayers and blessings over food were always said by his family at home. Yet, regardless how hard he prayed here, manna from heaven would not materialize.

The camp operated on two twelve-hour shifts. Chamush and his father were assigned to a maintenance crew that cleaned and painted the administrative quarters. Menek was assigned to a factory that made shells for the German rifles. His job initially was to sweep the factory floors and empty and wash the trash bins. Lifting the trash bins was a particular struggle for him. On two occasions, when the German supervisor observed him struggling with the trash bins he asked, "How old are you?" Menek snapped to attention and quickly answered, "I am twelve years old."

On the second occasion, when Menek repeated the same answer, the supervisor gave him a menacing look and responded with a loud "HAH!"

The second incident convinced Menek that he was in mortal danger and that he had to do something to increase his worth and thus avoid the possibility of being included on the elimination list. In this camp, children, the sick and intellectuals were among the most disposable commodities. The intellectuals, in particular, were dropping off like leaves on a windy day in autumn.

Menek therefore instinctively adopted several practices: he worked at double speed whenever any German SS were in the immediate vicinity; he did not allow the trash bins to fill up to the top; he did everything possible to be less visible to any decision-makers. And most importantly, he began teaching himself to operate a munitions-making machine. He knew it would make him more valuable. He could see that tradesmen, such as carpenters, electricians and mechanics, had a better chance at survival. Having a *"fach,"* a trade, made the difference between life and death.

With the help of a fellow inmate, whom Menek called the "Angel," he seized every opportunity to learn the operation of a shell-making machine. The "Angel" who helped him was a very gentle and patient man. He recognized the boy's drive to become indispensable. He even encouraged Menek to ask any and all questions.

The assembly line contained several machines that trimmed and grooved rifle shells, among many other types of shells. Each machine operator had to meet a specified quota. The consequences could be very dire if an operator did not meet his assigned quota, so lengthy or frequent visits to the latrine could put one at great risk. After having learned to operate a groove-making machine, Menek was eager to step in for any operator who temporarily had to leave his station. When he felt it was safe, the "Angel" invited Menek many times to practice his new skills on his machine.

On one such occasion, the German SS supervisor spotted Menek from a distance in the process of removing a jammed shell from a machine. One had to perform a partial disassembly of the machine, re-assemble it, re-calibrate the settings and perform an operational test. Menek accomplished all those steps flawlessly, without being aware that the supervisor was observing him. By that time, the nearby machine operators held their breath in anticipation of a deadly punishment about to be meted out to both the boy and the operator.

After restarting the machine, Menek turned to the left and observed the SS supervisor heading straight towards him. He began to tremble and felt his knees almost giving out from under him. Menek stood petrified, unable to move a single muscle. When the supervisor arrived at the station, he reached into the box of freshly cut shells, removed one, examined it carefully, measured its dimension and asked, "Do you know how to operate this machine?" Menek, still trembling, said "*Ya,*" to which he responded "*Gut*" and walked away. Menek heaved a sigh of relief. Had the supervisor been in a foul mood he would have killed both Menek and the operator for having taken this initiative without permission.

Skarzysko was a perfect breeding ground for typhus. Typhus-riddled men and women holding on to life were a commonplace sight in this camp. It killed thousands of prisoners. When Menek saw a man with red facial eruptions exhibiting a high fever, he knew that it would be just a matter of days in which the man would "no longer be here."

Typhus is a microorganism that is transmitted by lice between human beings. It occurs in areas where humans are crowded together under unsanitary conditions. The disease spreads rapidly, and in most instances, is fatal. The symptoms begin with mild headaches and a rash, eventually leading to red blemishes on the body, extremely high fever, confusion and ultimately, death. The whole process takes between ten to fourteen days.

Early one morning Menek happened to be sweeping the area near the "Angel." When he looked up at him he saw the man's face was covered with red blotches and that he was shaking with the chills that accompany high fever. That night, as Menek was lying in the top tier of his straw lined bunk bed next to his father and brother, he asked if there was anything they could do for that angelic man. His father said to pray for him, to ask God to bring him a speedy recovery. Menek prayed with all his might. The next morning, for the first time since he arrived in Skarzysko, he was actually anxious to get to work so that he could see his dear friend—only to find out that "he was no longer here."

Ask not for whom I say Kaddish.

The following day, as Menek prepared to take his clean-up position along with the rest of the maintenance crew, he was summoned to the German SS supervisor's office. He went into a state of panic. On his way to the office, a million thoughts raced around in his mind:

"He's going to shoot me because the SS found out that I lied about my age."
"I will get whipped because I worked on a machine when I was supposed to be sweeping the floor."
"I didn't clean up well enough yesterday."
"I am going to be shipped to Werk C and die a slow death."
"I'm going to be re-assigned to a work detail for outside duties in freezing temperatures. . ."

Menek marched in and came to a halt in front of a white line. He stood at attention. He knew that accidentally crossing that white line meant certain death. He had also learned that if he spoke before he was spoken to, the consequences could be disastrous.

The German SS supervisor stood at the window looking out into the yard, cracking his whip against his boot, and raising Menek's blood pressure to dizzying levels.

Two days earlier this very same butcher pulled out a pistol from its holster and without a word killed two men in the very same yard that his eyes were now scanning. The men that he killed committed the heinous crime of taking an unauthorized break.

When he finally spoke he said, "You will now operate a machine." He then paused for a few seconds and said, *"Raus!"*

His aide standing near the door motioned to Menek to follow him. They walked halfway down "Machine Lane," with Menek following a few steps behind the aide. When they finally came to a stop, the aide pointed to a shell-making machine and said, "This is your machine." Menek found himself standing in front of the "Angel's" machine.

Several weeks after their arrival in Skarzysko, Menek's father contracted typhus. One morning as everyone was getting ready to go to work, he complained that he did not have the strength to go. Against the advice of other inmates, he went off to the infirmary while everyone else went to work. That evening when the two brothers were eating their rations, a man joined by two witnesses said to them, "Your father is no longer here." He had been taken to the woods and unceremoniously shot.

There was no crying, no hysteria, just a motionless staring into space. But that night the two newly-made orphans held on to each other and cried quietly in each other's arms.

Menek reflected back to the days in Tarnobrzeg when he used to jump into his parents' bed. How he loved being sandwiched between them! He so desperately wanted to relive those moments again, but he knew that those days were gone forever. Utter exhaustion finally allowed him a few hours of sleep.

Not satisfied with just the words "he is no longer here," the two brothers searched for witnesses that might give them more details. Within a day or two, the full picture of their loss unfolded. On the day that their father went to the infirmary, the SS held an "Action," a round-up for execution. Prisoners that were found in their bunks, including those in the infirmary, were hauled away in a truck and taken into the woods.

Those that could not move, or walked with great difficulty, were shot on the spot. The others, including Menek's father, were ordered to run in a straight line, while the Germans were shooting at them from either side of the line. The witness was a member of the detail assigned to dig a mass grave for the victims. He concluded his testimony with the words, "Your father didn't suffer," meaning he died quickly.

Skarzysko was a place where anomalous human behavior on either side of the spectrum was commonplace. Inhumanity to man was often counterbalanced by acts of superhuman self-sacrifice. Even within the prisoner ranks, one could observe conduct that spanned the gamut of human behavior.

For example: an emaciated man, barely able to stand on his own feet, gave up a half slice of bread to his typhus-ridden friend, while a *"Kapo"*—a prisoner elevated to the rank of policeman—beat another blotch-riddled man for not moving fast enough for the line-up.

The German SS tried to select the lowest of the low from the ranks of Jewish prisoners to serve as their policemen inside the camp. Their job was to dole out the food, line up the prisoners, and supposedly keep order inside the camp. Most of the *Kapos* behaved decently. They acted harshly only when the Germans were watching. However, there were some *Kapos* who were truly vicious. They sold their souls, if they had any, for the extra portion of bread and soup.

Ukrainian soldiers were the principal guards around the perimeter of the camp. Some were criminals released from jails in order to do this dirty work for the Germans. Besides guarding Jewish prisoners, they were sometimes assigned to menial guard duty, such as marching prisoners from one place to another, or standing as sentry over work details. They, unlike the Germans, had blue uniforms that never looked neat. They were either too wrinkled or oversized. They had no pistols, only long rifles with fixed bayonets. They too, when given the opportunity, took pleasure in killing Jews indiscriminately.

Each ammunition factory was a beehive of rotating machinery. Huge motors drove long overhead drive shafts that spanned almost the full length of the factory building. Each drive shaft was equipped with a large array of pulleys. Each pulley in turn was strategically located directly over its respective machine. All the machines were thus driven by a vast array of leather belts that connected them to the rotating pulleys.

Leather belts, therefore, were considered a precious commodity. One was expected to make an effort to have a belt repaired if it broke. However, some belts became so worn out that the Germans did not consider them worth repairing.

When the winters became brutally cold, the prisoners used scrap leather to line their shoes. Many prisoners wore Dutch-made clogs. They were wooden shoes without inner linings. The leather provided an extra measure of protection against the cold. It also minimized bleeding ulcers, caused by constant rubbing of the naked feet against the wood. Menek too had to wear the clogs after his shoes deteriorated. His feet were particularly small. Even though he was given a small ladies shoe size, he was not spared from chronic bleeding and ulcerated feet.

It didn't take very long for the German bookkeepers to notice that the attrition rate of leather belts increased. Hence, an edict was issued from the top: "Any prisoner caught with even the smallest piece of leather will be shot."

To set an example, the following week, all prisoners were forced to assemble at the *"Appelplatz,"* the prisoner assembly grounds, to watch a public execution of a man who was caught with a piece of leather.

By that time, seeing a man transported from life to death in just a matter of seconds was no longer a novelty to either Chamush or Menek. After such episodes Chamush and Menek clung to each other in their lice-riddled, straw-lined, urine-stained, third-tier wooden shelf. The mornings were particularly difficult for the two brothers. Each worried about the other's welfare and safe return to the barrack.

Even though Menek was assigned to a productive machine, he never felt safe away from the factory. The plant provided a small measure of security because it gave him the opportunity to demonstrate that he was worth keeping alive. However, during the periods that he was not at work, mortal danger lurked at every turn. He was short and gaunt and did not portray, to the Germans, an image of being a useful cost-effective tool.

One cold, rainy day all the prisoners were ordered to assemble at the *Appelplatz*. The assembly was called at a very unusual time. After everyone stood on the assembly grounds for several hours in a cold driving rain, the commandant made an announcement: "Two prisoners are missing, and since they have not been found, the rest of you will have to be punished." The Germans took pleasure in collective punishment.

The punishment was ten dead Jews for every missing prisoner. The "selection" of sacrificial lambs was not totally indiscriminate. The most likely candidates were the weak and the very young.

A German SS officer, followed by two rifle toting SS soldiers, walked down the rows of lined up prisoners and sporadically stopped, pointed to a prisoner and said, *"Raus!"*

When he came down the row in which Menek and Chamush were standing, he stopped in front of Menek, pointed to the boy next to him and said, *"Raus!"* After the rain-soaked prisoners were dismissed, the twenty chosen sacrificial lambs were marched into the woods and shot.

Ask not for whom I say Kaddish.

Menek was forever planning, calculating, measuring and weighing every available option for every situation that might spell danger. He seized on every opportunity to enhance his value as a worker.

One day the machine operator adjacent to Menek was seen by the German SS supervisor with a piece of leather sticking out his wooden shoe. The man was marched out in front of all the prisoners and taken to the back of the factory building. A shot was heard and he "was no longer here."

Within the hour the foreman of that section walked over to Menek and asked him if he was able to temporarily operate both machines. And to show his "charity," he said, "You don't have to meet your quota on the second machine."

Without hesitation, Menek responded that he was able to operate two machines simultaneously. Menek took it even a step further. By the end of the day he was able to demonstrate that both machines were on the way to meeting their respective quotas.

The next day when the SS supervisor was making his rounds, the foreman showed him Menek's talent. He observed him, grinned, and said grudgingly, *"Der kleiner Jude,* the little Jew." Menek felt a little bit safer.

From that day forward, whenever Nazi delegations and various dignitaries were taken on inspection tours of the factory, Menek's station was one of the key stops. Sometimes he was ordered to demonstrate his ability to dismantle certain portions of a machine and reassemble it while being timed. The SS supervisor usually boasted how he was able to train "this little Jew."

Ultimately, these demonstrations created a terrible inner conflict in Menek. He felt like a traitor because he understood that his work contributed to the German war machine, but he also realized that this work was keeping him alive. And so, on those days when life in camp was unbearable and indiscriminate killings reached an intolerable level, Menek turned to sabotage.

The machine that he was operating performed two functions. The first was to trim the end of the shell to a specified length. The second function was to cut a precision groove at the back-end of the shell, around its circumference. The purpose of the groove was to facilitate an effective grip on the shell, so that when the rifle was fired, the bullet could exit the barrel without the shell. The depth of the groove had to be precise. If it was too shallow, the clamp would not grip the shell and it would move down the barrel along with the bullet and consequently jam the rifle. If the groove was too deep, the powder would explode in the breech of the rifle, rendering it useless and likely injure the shooter. On a number of occasions Menek deliberately adjusted the groove cut to be either shallow or deep, as did other operators. If any operator was ever caught deliberately producing a single shell that did not meet calibration standards, it meant certain and immediate death.

One particular day, Menek felt as if he had reached the end of his rope. The clogs had caused his feet to bleed again. So when he arrived at the factory he removed them and worked in his bare feet on a freezing cold factory floor. Then he stepped on a hot shell, which burned the bottom of his foot. Early that morning he saved half his portion of bread so that he could have it later in the day, only to have it stolen out from under him. A gut-wrenching hunger made him feel weak the whole day. And the night before, they had to stand on the *Appelplatz* for hours because the prisoner count did not tally. He became overwhelmed with unadulterated hatred for the Germans and was driven to strike back. "This time they are going to pay dearly," he said to himself.

His eyes scanned the factory floor very quickly. He wanted to make sure that an inspector was not in the area. When he felt it was safe, he swung back to his machine and adjusted the groove cut to an unacceptably shallow level. His spirits gradually soared with visions of German soldiers fighting on the front lines with jammed rifles. His empty stomach stilled its complaint and the nerve-ends at the bottom of his feet fell silent.

Menek allowed his machine to spit out hundreds of rejects into a large wooden box. The taste of revenge was too sweet to alter course. The accepted practice was just a few rejects, because the chances were small of an inspector picking out a bad shell out of hundreds of good shells. Even if one or two bad shells were found they could be explained away as a problem with the cutting bit. However, Menek kept filling the box with bad shells, while nervously scanning the factory floor.

At some point he stopped the machine and readjusted the settings to obtain the proper groove depth. By that time the box was half full and most of the shells were rejects. As soon as he restarted his machine, Menek spotted the inspector making his rounds. He knew that by the time the inspector would arrive at his station, the box would contain only a few good shells.

His heart began to race and he broke out in a cold sweat. His whole body was shaking by the time the inspector came to a stop at his machine. The inspector reached into the box with his left hand and pulled out a handful of shells. He then allowed all of them to fall back into the box, except one. He placed his right hand into the pocket of his white lab coat and removed a pair of calipers, a measuring device.

Menek died a thousand deaths in that short period of time. Would he find a good shell or one of the hundreds of bad ones? He was delirious with terror. He began to imagine what it would feel like when the inevitable bullet entered his body. Until that moment, Menek had already seen hundreds of decaying corpses and dozens of summary executions, but in his mind he had always been able to rationalize that it was "they, not I." Now he was staring into the stark reality that it was "I." This time, it is "I" who will be looking down into the barrel of a gun, he thought. He already saw himself on the "other side," joining his father, Bubby and Zaidy, his uncles, aunts and cousins.

The inspector took his time, checking out the integrity of the one shell left in his hand. When he finished he looked at Menek and said, "*Sehr gut,* very good," and continued on his way down the line.

The Skarzysko concentration camp shall forever live in infamy.

Chapter Four

A Muted Welcome

Menek's mother, at age thirty-seven, suddenly discovered that she was a widow. The news reached her several months after her husband's death. The thought of her children being alone put her into a panic. She had an acquaintance from Tarnobrzeg who was an administrative assistant in *Werk A*. He was sent to *Werk B* to perform several administrative tasks. His work required him to go back and forth several times. She learned from him, after one of his visits, that a maintenance group of builders and painters was being formed to erect new German SS office barracks in *Werk A*.

She immediately began turning heaven and earth to be transferred to *Werk A*. She made contact with several prison administrative assistants, including the one from Tarnobrzeg, beseeching each and every one of them to shuffle papers and documents to effect a transfer for her and Hanue. After much manipulation, and the efforts by a few good souls, their names eventually appeared on the list of experienced painters to be transferred to *Werk A*.

The boys were not aware of all the efforts that their mother was making to get to them. At about the same time, Menek contracted typhus. He woke up one morning with a severe headache and a high fever. He said nothing to his brother, but instead got himself ready for the line-up and the morning ration. He mechanically consumed his slice of black bread and a tin cup of black coffee. He was grateful to see only a few red spots on his body and that the fever did not debilitate him. However, as the day wore on, he became increasingly weaker. Making adjustments to his machine became physically more taxing. His body grew hotter with each passing hour. By the end of the twelve-hour shift, he was in the throes of a full-blown typhus battle. He had already learned that showing any signs of weakness could be fatal. He therefore took extra precautions to be minimally visible.

When he woke the following morning, his body was on fire with fever. He was dizzy and unable to focus his eyes on anything. He recognized the seriousness of the situation. For the first time since he arrived in Skarzysko, his stomach-twisting hunger was gone. Nonetheless, he forced himself to get on line for the morning ration. A sure sign of one's imminent demise was when the prisoner no longer made an attempt to get food.

Menek knew his chances of survival were minimal if he stayed in the barrack. He was also certain that if he went to the infirmary, that as a small boy, he would be judged as unproductive and thus be destined for the "garbage heap." He concluded that his best chance was the factory. The big problem, of course, was the march to and from the factory. It was about a half-mile walk, but on that morning, the distance seemed infinite. He willed himself to line up for the march to the plant. Would he be able to walk past the guards? Would he be able to walk a straight line? Prayer had already lost its polish for him.

The prisoners generally marched in rows of five. Two men that worked with Menek at nearby machines became very helpful. They placed Menek in the middle of a row and held him up as they marched past the Ukrainian guards. At one checkpoint a guard noticed them, but quickly looked away.

Once in the factory, Menek was able to operate the machine, but with great difficulty. But he knew better then to attempt to make any repairs to the machine if it jammed. In the dizzy state that he was in, he could have lost one or two fingers if he tried. Again, the two men at the adjacent machines helped him out. They took turns removing jams for him. These were the same men that Menek helped when he was first learning to operate the machines. He had stood in for them so that they could take longer breaks.

The high fever, chills, nausea, and dizziness persisted for several days. Each succeeding day made the march between the camp and factory more torturous. Menek refused to give into the disease. On several occasions the plant SS men observed his acutely sick state without comment. They did not consider it a problem, so long as the operator met his quota.

Menek woke up one morning ravenously hungry. His fever dropped precipitously. He became one of a very few that beat that sinister disease. It was just another battle in the war for ultimate survival.

In late May, a bright morning sun finally made its early appearance in the East. The blue skies nudged aside the April clouds. Singing birds, rarely ever seen inside the camp, were perched on the barrack rooftop as a warm breeze announced the dawn of a new day. Menek's thoughts once again turned to earlier days of home. He longed for a day that would bring him back to his familiar garden-filled courtyard. He missed his family, his walks with his father, and the carefree summer days at the Visla river-edge. He recalled the holidays and the Friday nights when his father embraced him and his brother, and said the traditional prayer:

> May the Lord bless you and protect you,
> May the Lord shine His countenance on you and be gracious to you,
> May the Lord turn His countenance to you and bring you peace.

He could not wrench himself away from thoughts of those days. It was so difficult for him to accept the reality of things as they were. He gradually came to understand that those days were gone forever. He stopped asking "why," and instead began doubting if there would ever be a "when." At the age of ten, Menek had become an old man.

By the time their mother arrived in *Werk A,* the boys had fallen into a camp routine. They formed an unbreakable bond. They learned to trust in each other and in the bond that held them together. Hence, her arrival did not change things much. Rather, it was she who needed to be near her children, or so it seemed to Menek.

The boys had already learned that the protection of a parent from the Nazis was completely ineffective. Menek, in particular, harbored an inner resentment against his parents because they failed to avert the calamity that had befallen the family. Therefore, her arrival did not raise much excitement for him. He was conflicted with mixed emotions.

Once again with the help of the administrative assistant, she was able to have the boys moved from the men's barracks to her barrack. Menek found it a little difficult at first to adjust to the different dynamics that existed in the women's barracks. The conversations were significantly different. There were additional restrictions placed upon him and his brother. For example, they had to remember not to go to the women's latrine, but instead walk a longer distance to the men's area. When the women were undressing, the boys were instructed to look elsewhere. Menek discovered at an early age the phenomenon of the menstrual cycle. The emotional pain that young women displayed when they stopped menstruating—a relatively common occurrence in the camp—puzzled him.

One night Menek was wakened by the cries of a newborn baby. He was startled both by the cries and by the fact that there was a baby in the barrack. He never saw a baby in any of the barracks before. He knew that the Nazis killed them before they even got to the camp. When he tried to get out of his rack to see the baby, his mother pulled him back and said, "Don't look and don't go there." He had already learned by this time that such a comment required no further explanation. The cries were heard throughout the barrack and nobody moved a muscle. Many women sobbed quietly as they held their palms against their ears. The following morning when Menek got out of his rack to go to the latrine, he saw a small infant, with the umbilical chord still attached, lying dead on the cold ground.

Chamush's restless sleep habits got worse, and so did his talking in his sleep. On a couple of occasions he walked in his sleep. He went to the latrine without knowing that he did so. Once he even wound up returning to a different rack. When Menek recalled the time they spent hiding in the haystack, he was thankful that his parents had dismissed that plan. Even the camp latrines could spell danger for a small-framed sleepwalker like his brother.

The latrine was nothing more then a large building frame built over a trench-like, oval-shaped pit. The floor inside the building contained about forty evenly spaced holes, small enough for an adult to straddle, but too large and precarious for a small boy. The pit was about twenty feet wide, fifty to sixty feet long, and about six feet deep. One end of the pit was exposed so that a septic tank wagon pulled by prisoners could be positioned and the bucket-wielding brigade (known as the "shit brigade") could fill it up with the raw sewage. If one was not careful, especially in the dark of night, one could easily fall into the pit. The unremitting stench emanating from the area was generally sufficient warning that one was approaching the open pit. Was that enough to deter a sleepwalker? His worries for Chamush persisted.

Eventually, Menek's mother and brother ended up working together in the same maintenance division. Their work consisted principally of cleaning and painting the German SS quarters and offices. Each had learned their respective tasks. Therefore, as long as they were productive, and didn't fall into the hands of an arbitrary and capricious monster, their survival was relatively assured. The omnipresent dangers such as typhus, "selections," and merciless beatings still remained. But one learned to live with these ubiquitous threats.

Menek continued his work in the ammunition factory and he became the "must see" attraction for all German SS visitors to the plant. On many such occasions, he was ordered to demonstrate his ability to operate two machines simultaneously.

One of the men that Menek befriended was known as "Jacob the Learned." Jacob was someone who was treated with a lot of respect by the many prisoners who knew him. A tall man in his early fifties, he was highly educated and carried himself with an air of dignity. Jacob had arrived on a transport with his wife and three teenaged children. His wife and daughter were sent to *Werk B,* and his two sons were shipped off to *Werk C.* He was assigned to the clean-up crew around the factory that Menek had originally been a part of. He was very comforting to Menek immediately after he lost his father.

Jacob said very little, but he was a good listener and observer. On numerous occasions small groups of people gathered around him to get his opinions on current events or his interpretations on happenings in the camp. He was a very compassionate man, even with people he hardly knew. He never got used to the sight of corpses piled high in the boxes. He truly felt the loss of every human being.

Every man's death diminishes me.

On the day when he received word that both of his sons died in *Werk C,* Jacob collapsed onto the floor and literally had to be revived by his fellow inmates. A number of people surrounded him and attempted to comfort him, but he was inconsolable for several hours. After he wiped his eyes and regained his composure, he looked hard into the face of every man that his eyes could capture and issued a command in full voice to them all:

"Just as it is every Jew's responsibility to retell the story of the Exodus from Egypt, so it will be *your* responsibility—and the responsibility of every single survivor—to tell the world of the horrors that took place here."

He spoke with such passion that his words felt like they came from Mount Sinai. Menek would not forget them.

Later he implored everyone not to let his wife find out about their sons, even if it meant telling her a lie. He was convinced that she would never survive the news. Several months later, his wife and daughter succumbed to typhus and soon they too "were no longer here."

And so now everyone lied to him. Nevertheless, Jacob the Learned gradually became withdrawn, incommunicative and emotionally shriveled. Seeing the slow deterioration in his adopted hero was especially devastating to Menek. Jacob had been an unyielding buoy, an anchor in the midst of a violent storm. Now, he too was broken.

Most slave laborers ultimately lost their perception of progressively marked time. The prisoner existed from one close call to the next, from selection to selection. A "selection" meant a line-up of camp inmates for the sole purpose of weeding out "unfit" prisoners. Selections were generally held when a new harvest of prisoners was brought to the camp, or when typhus produced an unusually large crop of weak and sick people. They were the most dreaded and dehumanizing events in the camp. It was a time when the very young would run and hide. Regardless of the temperature, prisoners—men and women—were made to strip completely and forced to advance naked in single file in front of German SS "doctors" in white coats. Any inmates with blemishes on their body, or any prisoners who appeared sick or weak, were "selected" for disposal. One of the men who was exceptionally helpful to Menek when he was besieged with typhus was "selected" and "eliminated."

Who shall live and who shall die.

Seasons came and went, and Menek survived his eleventh birthday. His survival is also partially due to the charity of a Polish free worker, a young woman who was paid for her labor and free to go home after work. She worked at a leather sewing machine across the main isle and diagonally opposite Menek's station.

Several months after his bout with typhus, she gathered the courage and greeted him one day with a quick hello. The Polish workers were not permitted to speak to the Jewish prisoners. And certainly, the prisoners were never allowed to speak to anyone. She worked ten hours a day, in contrast to the twelve-hour shifts of the slave laborers. She was free to come and go according to a schedule that was set up for the small number of Polish workers employed by the Germans.

She generally ate her lunch, which she brought from home, at her machine. Menek unknowingly was unable to take his eyes off her whenever she ate. The unrelenting hunger removed all inhibitions and he was completely unaware that he was transfixed on her eating. She must have felt his penetrating gaze. And so one day when she finished her lunch, she looked over to Menek and pointed to a piece of cake that she left over. She then got up and went to the washroom.

Menek looked in all directions, to make sure that it was safe and then he scurried across the isle, snatched the piece of cake and devoured it before he returned to his machine. When she returned, he gave her a grateful nod and she just smiled. A few days later she left him a half of an apple. Most of the times if she left anything over, it consisted of cookies or cake. One day Menek mustered the courage to ask for bread or a potato instead of pastry. From that time on, Menek got his wish. Two to three times a week he was able to consume either an extra slice of bread or a cold potato. This life-saving good fortune lasted for several months. One day, without any notice, she was moved out of the factory. The days of Menek's "extra snack" were over.

In the early spring of 1944, the camp became significantly more crowded. The early German victories on the Eastern front were turning into defeats. It seemed as if each setback caused the SS to be more vicious. The number of beatings and arbitrary shootings, for the slightest infraction, increased considerably. Even healthy specimen and experienced tradesmen lost their consumable value. It became the worst of times inside the camp. Yet buoyed by the news that the war was going badly for the Germans, many of the operators, including Menek, were emboldened to engage in sabotage, even though few believed that they would survive to see the light of freedom again. Nevertheless, the instinct for self-preservation dictated a high degree of caution during those times when he and the others ran their machines out of the set specifications. Menek had just finished doing his part when he spotted an old bunkmate running towards him, furiously flailing his arms. When he came to a stop he blurted out, "Your mother and brother are being marched into the woods to be shot."

His mother and brother were part of a large contingent assigned to clean and paint German office barracks. Several members in their group, which consisted of about forty to fifty people, were accused of taking an unauthorized break. As a "reprimand," the German SS decided to kill every person in that group. And so they were ordered to line up for a long march into the woods. Word spread of this very quickly amongst the prisoners.

Menek stopped his machine as his eyes began to frantically search the factory floor for the German SS commander of the plant. The commander's rank was sufficiently high to potentially countermand most low rank SS officers' orders. In a frenzied state Menek ran between machines, searching and screaming his name. He gave no thought to caution as he ran out of the factory without permission, in search of the commander. Jacob the Learned, who rarely spoke anymore, was cleaning up an area between two buildings as Menek ran by him. When he deciphered the reason for Menek's panic, he stopped him and calmly said, "The butcher is on his way back into the factory."

By the time Menek returned to the factory floor, he was completely out of breath. He had not cried in years, but now the tears were streaming down his face as he came to a stop in front of the SS commander.

Menek had already committed two serious crimes punishable by death. First, he left his machine and the factory floor without permission. Second, he had the impudence to approach a German officer without being so ordered. And now he was about to commit an equally serious crime by speaking to a German officer before being spoken to. His laser-sharp glare and the crack of the whip against his boot did not stop Menek from crying out, "They are going to shoot my mother and my brother! I have no one left in my family. Please help me!"

The commander stood there for a few seconds somewhat confused, not quite sure if he should kill this impudent little Jew, strike him with his whip, or help him. Menek had taken the gamble, knowing that even though he was a butcher, he would not kill him, because Menek made him look good to the visiting dignitaries. The best he could hope for was to save the remnant of his family and subsequently receive a fierce whipping. Another serious offense committed by Menek was his daring to look him directly in the eye, adding the words, "We have very little time to save them."

The SS commander looked at his watch and abruptly said, "Follow me."

He walked out into the factory yard, with Menek following behind him. He then motioned to his driver to come quickly to his car that was parked near the front door. He and his driver got into the automobile as he instructed Menek to stand on the running board, but not to touch the upholstery.

The woods were about three to four kilometers from the factory. The time to get there seemed to Menek like an eternity. Terrifying thoughts raced through his mind as he stood on that running board. He could not picture a life without them. He held his breath as he heard shots ring out in the distance. Several people were already lying motionless on the ground as the car pulled up to the shooting gallery.

The SS commander yelled "Halt!" and the shooters stopped. He then walked over to the officer in charge and said something. A moment later he called Menek to come forward and said, "Show me your mother and brother."

They were still standing as Menek pointed them out. The two were ordered to step out of the firing line.

As a Ukrainian soldier began leading his mother and brother back to camp, the officer yelled, "Resume firing." Menek was ordered to step back onto the running board of the car. No words were exchanged and within minutes he was back at his machine. That night when the lights went out and they climbed into the rack, they all held on to each other a little tighter.

The summer brought with it comforting warm temperatures. Going to and from work in the daylight made the hardship a little more bearable. Even the incessant hunger seemed more tolerable. Yet the periodic dreams of feasts and holiday dinners never stopped. Dreams of home and the tranquillity of Saturday afternoons with family were generally shattered by a wake-up call and the stark reality of camp. But one could not allow oneself the luxury of self-pity. Self-pity was a first step to throwing in the towel. And once a man or woman did that, then it was just a matter of time before they too joined "the here no more's."

Menek had a recurrent dream. He dreamt that he was walking with his mother in the Zakopane Woods. In the late winter just before the war, his mother had taken ill. The illness lingered into the early spring. The doctor suggested she go to a warmer climate with better air. The Carpathian Mountains were well known for their healing powers. Since Menek was very attached to her, she would not consider going without him. And so she took him with her as she went with a group of her friends to a place called Zakopane.

Zakopane, before the war, was a small resort town located south of Krakow near Poland's southernmost border, in the middle of the Carpathian Mountains. The rolling hills and meandering tree-lined paths, dotted with thousands of colorful plants and flowers, created a perfect setting for poets. The scenery and sweet scent of nature's bountiful beauty brought out the music in the visitor's soul. This was a place created by God to inspire painters and composers.

So it was in this setting that Menek's mother strolled with her friends, holding his hand as they sang a Yiddish song, "Between the Golden Stalks." The melody was even more beautiful than the scenery. His mother's lovely face completed the exquisiteness of the scenery.

When she looked down at her son with her warm smile, while adding harmony to the melody, she completed his personal Garden of Eden. Even at the young and tender age of six, Menek was able to absorb and forever file away those warm memories of his Garden of Eden. And so when some days in Skarzysko were particularly bad, Menek forced his mind to reflect back to Zakopane and internally sang to himself "Between the Golden Stalks."

In the middle of July 1944, word spread in the camp that the Russian front was getting closer. As hope of freedom increased among many prisoners, so did the pleas from those who were dying—"not to forget them to the world, so that their deaths would not be in vain."

This theme was repeated in every barrack. Menek was not yet mentally prepared to think of a life after Skarzysko. He had already experienced too many disappointments. Two opposing rumors floated around in the camp. One was that the Russians would soon liberate the camp. The other, spoken only in hushed words, was that the German SS would exterminate all the Jews in the camp, in order to get rid of the evidence. The beautiful summer weather did very little to blunt the sting of uncertainty.

Early one morning all the prisoners were ordered to report to the *Appelplatz*. The *Kapos* and several SS soldiers with their dogs were sent into the barracks to make sure they were emptied. Trucks were brought in to haul away those who did not get out of their racks and those who were in the infirmary. The German SS were out in force, including all of their German shepherd dogs. The men were made to stand on one half of the assembly grounds and the women on the other. After more than an hour, and after the count was verified in accordance with the German penchant for exactness, four long tables and chairs were brought out and placed about twenty feet apart. The prisoners were then herded together into two large groups. The camp commandant announced that most inmates would be shipped to another camp.

And so the "Great Selection" began. The *Kapos* were ordered to bring the prisoners to the tables in groups of fifty. Four groups were formed, two from the men's side and two from the women's. When the respective groups were brought within several hundred feet of the tables, the prisoners were ordered to strip and form single lines leading to each table. Each table had three German SS. The one in the middle wore a white coat. The other two were sharply dressed in their SS uniforms, with pistols neatly tucked into their holsters and their razor-sharp whips neatly placed on top of the tables. Behind each table stood two SS soldiers with machine guns at the ready. The whole *Appelplatz* was ringed with heavily armed SS soldiers, German shepherd dogs and their handlers. As the prisoners approached the table they heard from the man in the white coat only one of two words, either "Left" or "Right."

Who shall live, and who shall die.

The weak, the sick, and the worn out were ordered to the Left. The others were sent to the Right. The selection continued in the hot sun into the late afternoon.

Throughout this process Menek and his brother hung on to each other without uttering a word. Finally their turn came to fall into a single line. They stripped naked, rolled up their striped uniforms and waited for their turn. Menek stood two paces behind his brother. It was a hot summer day but Menek became unexpectedly cold. He willed himself not to tremble and not to show weakness or fear. He saw some people praying silently while others were bordering on delirium. He no longer relied on, nor did he believe in prayer. He just stood there staring at the German SS sitting at the table. He suddenly felt all alone.

As his brother stepped forward, all his senses funneled into his eardrums. He heard the life-granting sound, "RIGHT." Buoyed by what he heard, Menek thus stepped forward confidently and briskly to once again hear, "RIGHT." As they rejoined the group of the living, the two brothers once again held on to each other very tightly.

By this time hunger and thirst reared their ugly heads again. The tension in the air had momentarily held their stomachs at bay. Chamush and Menek immediately turned to focus their eyes in the direction of the women. They scanned the "living" group first. Menek could not bring himself to look in the direction of the other group. Instead he fixed his eyes on the lines that had not as yet been examined.

He spotted Hanue first, and immediately in front of her, his mother. As he looked at his mother, his heart overflowed with love and admiration for her. Dressed or undressed, she stood erect with aristocratic poise, looking as beautiful as ever. He knew she was not a reject. She was his mother!

The two brothers were transfixed on the two women, oblivious to anything that may have gone on around them. Very few words passed between them as each tightened his grip on the other's hand. For a split second, when Menek took his eyes off his mother, he realized that he and his brother were the only two still naked amongst a group of men who were already dressed. A few minutes later Hanue and his mother were standing with the group of the "living." The tension in Menek's body dissipated very slowly.

The two boys put on their striped pants and jackets and retreated back into the crowd. Menek's clothes were several sizes too big. His jacket, as well as the jackets of the other prisoners, had two large letters, "KL," painted in white on the back. The KL stood for "Concentration Camp" in German. Having to stand in the hot sun in heavy clothes, compounded by the onslaught of thirst and hunger, made Menek very weak. He momentarily leaned on his brother to regain his balance.

This was a time of the year when children in other parts of the world were playing in parks, swimming in pools, lakes, and beaches. It was a time when couples were promising their eternal love to one another. A time for barbeques and picnics with family and friends. A time for lovers to take long walks in the cool shade of the woods. A time for parents and grandparents to watch their progeny perform on outdoor theater stages. A time for children to be going to summer camp. But for the Jews in Skarzysko, it was a never-ending struggle for continued corporal existence.

Several dirt hauling trucks rolled onto the *Appelplatz* as soon as the selection was finished. Their rear tailgates were dropped open and the people that went to the "Left" were now ordered, with the help of saliva-streaming German shepherd dogs, to squeeze like sardines onto the rear platforms. This process took less then thirty minutes and then within the blink of an eye the trucks with their cargo were gone.

Ask not for whom I say Kaddish.

The prisoners that remained standing were told that they were being shipped to two other labor camps. The women were to go to an all women's camp and the men to an all men's camp.

The order was given to form five-man rows. As the men were lining up, Menek and his brother anxiously scanned their eyes back and forth at the columns of women marchers being formed, but they could not pick out their mother. The best that the two brothers could do was a wave in that direction as they were being marched out to the railroad depot outside the camp.

Chapter Five

The Train Ride

The march to the railroad depot was filled with new tension. The depot was several kilometers from the camp. For the prisoners, the tension grew in intensity with each passing kilometer. Menek's contingent consisted of several hundred men. Each group was guarded by an unusually large number of SS soldiers.

Countless rumors regarding the true destination for the prisoners began to circulate at the speed of light. The most prevalent was that the transport was destined for an extermination camp. The theory was that the selection process was merely a ploy to avert possible chaos.

A railroad siding at the depot held a long chain of boxcars. There were no visible locomotives attached to either end of the train. Each boxcar contained two large sliding doors on opposite sides. One door was fully open; the other was cracked open about six inches and locked in that position. Each boxcar was designed with two miniature windows, both covered over with steel bars, located diagonally opposite each other and situated near the interior roof.

The station was lined with heavily armed soldiers and dogs. They surrounded the whole train as far as the eye could see. The SS officers held their whips at the ready; the snarling dogs were poised for action too.

The prisoners were marched to the open door sides of the cattle cars and ordered to stop. Within a few minutes the senior SS officer blew a whistle and all hell broke loose. The dogs, the whips, the kicking, screaming and beatings, accompanied the order to board the train. The prisoners were herded like beasts into the boxcars. Pandemonium broke out among the reluctant passengers as the whips were more generously applied. SS officers fired their pistols to encourage the still unconvinced passengers to enter.

As the cars filled up and captives cried that there was no more room, the SS fired their weapons across the open doors. This caused the prisoners to scramble away from the open doors, trampling over one another to avoid a bullet. And so more bodies were packed like sardines into the boxcars. The doors were then closed, leaving a small open slot for air. The German SS art of "high density packaging."

Menek and his brother held on to each other as they were being squeezed against the wall. Jacob the Learned was near them. He made a little space for them near the door slot. The sun had been beating down on them all day. The selection process and the march to the station had taken its toll even on the healthiest of men. Prayers for water and shade were unanimous and audible. But getting out of the sun and into the hot, breezeless boxcar was like going from the frying pan into the fire. The July sun on that day was relentless.

The train with its human cargo stood at the station till late that night. As midnight approached, a locomotive was hooked onto the cars and the train began its slow journey. By that time several people had passed out and regained consciousness; Jacob was one of them. When he was able to speak, he said out loud to everyone in hearing distance: "Remember, whoever survives must make it his duty to tell the world what happened here!"

The night air brought a little relief and the motion of the train added a life-saving breeze. Because Menek was small, he was able to stretch his feet, unlike many others. He was therefore able to sleep intermittently.

By mid-afternoon the following day the car had taken on the stench of urine and excrement. Only those men that were near the door slots were able to urinate out the doors. The car was too packed to allow to and fro movement. By the end of the second day, the cry for food changed to a steady, unanimous moan for water. Neither food nor water was given to the prisoners.

Periodically the train was diverted onto a railroad siding to allow other trains to pass. Those trains carried more valuable cargo, such as tanks and artillery. One time the human cargo gave way to livestock—pigs and cattle. They were certainly more valuable to the Germans than the Skarzysko expendables.

Each time the train was diverted and stopped, the guards surrounded it and allowed no one near. On such occasions, the door slot allowed Menek the opportunity to experience a panoramic view of the countryside. It offered him scenes beyond his immediate environment, providing him with views of an almost forgotten "normal" life outside the boxcar.

Birds—free, free birds—circled the open sky, unimpeded by man-made traps. The true concept of freedom was played out in front of his eyes. He desperately wished that he could be transformed into a bird. He saw lush green fields and rolling green meadows. His eyes became fixed on animals grazing in the shade of huge leaf-rich trees. Yet he and his fellow prisoners wallowed in a desolate field of human misery. This was the very antithesis of freedom! The antithesis of inner peace! Again he was tormented by the questions: "Why me?" "Why us?" "Where is God?"

God had seemed to join in the conspiracy against the human cargo. He used one hand to draw the sun closer to the train, and with the other hand, pushed the clouds away. The heat was barely tolerable as long as the train was in motion, but when it stood still, it became unbearable. Menek turned to Jacob to point out something he saw in the distance, but Jacob did not respond. His lifeless body lay next to Menek, with his mouth wide open but never to speak or reason again. His eyes were wide open too, but never to see or interpret a scene again.

Menek became angry with Jacob because he gave up. Why didn't he fight to stay alive, so that he could tell the world? He had the gift to speak, to write, to clarify and to elucidate. No one, Menek thought, could describe this Dante's Inferno better than Jacob. Now his inner rage would not subside. One more of Menek's anchors plummeted into the deep canyon. He looked at his brother without uttering a word. He realized he was looking at his remaining world, embodied in his brother. In silence, his eyes remained locked on Chamush's face.

Menek put his head down, closed his eyes and hoped for sleep, an escape that gave him the ability to cope. Sleep often brought dreams—dreams of former years, of home, of family and lots and lots of food. The dreams were varied, but among his favorite were memories of Friday nights and Saturdays.

On Friday nights, his home was beautifully illuminated. The Sabbath candles glowed as brightly as the radiant faces around the table. The traditional song of greeting, *"Sholom Aleichem,"* meaning "peace unto you," rang out throughout the house when the men returned home from the synagogue. The parents and grandparents blessed the children with every conceivable good wish. Songs and cheer were in abundance as the family brought in the Sabbath. The house smelled of freshly baked Sabbath breads intertwined with the aroma of mouthwatering cooked delicacies. The meals were intermingled with songs, quotes from the Bible, and bits of Jewish learning. A favorite text was *Pirke Avot,* "The Ethics of the Fathers." Gaiety and peace permeated the house throughout the Sabbath, right into Saturday night.

On Saturday night, candles were lit once again to bring in the new week. Each and every light in every room of the house was then turned on. Immediately thereafter, the whole family danced around the dining room table singing, "Good week, good week, let there be a good week!" The doors were thrown open for family and neighbors, who usually came to visit. And of course, the favorite visitor for Menek was Uncle Ephraim. The warmth of those nights was forever embedded in Menek's heart.

Those dreams recharged his batteries and gave him the coping mechanism that he needed to "hold on." But the "charged batteries" drained much too rapidly when he woke up and realized once more where he was.

A feeling of imminent doom hung over the human cargo when neither food nor water was given to them by the third day. It suggested to most of the passengers that they were on their way to an extermination camp. Jacob was "no longer here" to offer a well thought-out analysis of various possibilities. Gradually the parched passengers in the boxcar began to lose their voices, as they concurrently lost all hope. The cattle car took on an eerie silence punctuated periodically with feeble moans. Some just closed their eyes, checked out and went to the eternal Garden of Eden.

Menek still wanted to believe in the ultimate Garden of Eden for those who were wronged in this life, but he feared this too might be an unfathomable cruel joke. What if this too was a lie, an unthinkable sadistic ploy played on the minds of adhering believers? Were these thoughts that an eleven-year-old from a religious home should be having, he wondered.

Late in the night the train was again brought to a stop at a railroad siding near a small lake. The brutality of it all, thought Menek—to be looking at a body of fresh water, as human beings in boxcars were departing this world for the lack thereof.

The lake was peaceful and calm. The full moon that reflected off the tranquil water was blind to the nearby anguish, only a few hundred feet away. The summer's night song of crickets and frogs was drowned out by a symphony of human moans, interspersed with cries of "water, water." This was a new world symphony produced by the Nazi bastards, the heirs of Bach, Brahms, and Beethoven.

Menek was delirious with thoughts of cool, clean water. Whether he was awake or dozing, his brain pounded incessantly on his body to feed it water. Both he and his brother became very weak by the third day. He could not bring himself to drink his own urine, as did some of the others in the boxcar. When the train came to a brief stop in a small German town, Menek noticed children playing. He was no longer envious of their freedom. All he could see was a small puddle of stagnant water.

He and his brother gave each other courage to hold on. When one began to show signs of defeat, the other provided hope and encouragement. They turned to talk of their mother and expressed the conviction that they would some day be together again. They leaned on each other like two parched twigs in the midst of a howling desert storm.

By late afternoon on the third day the train arrived at its destination. The box-car doors were opened and the prisoners were ordered to disembark. To encourage the process, the Germans turned on several hoses of water at the base of the station platform. The water hose, meant to irrigate the desiccated mass of skeletal relics, was only several hundred feet away, but seemed like an infinite distance from the train.

Menek and Chamush, along with many prisoners staggered over to the hose, but many could not even make it to the water. And so as soon as the first group took their drinks, they brought back the life-saving nectar, in their tin cups, to those that could not move. Too many, however, were beyond the need for water. Among the living, the focus on water was so intense that the new arrivals did not immediately see their new home. The sign read, "Buchenwald."

The evolution of man is earth's saddest experiment.
Man seems to be the only living creature that is both carnivorous and sadistic.
He is capable of creating technology that can extend his reach beyond his
own galaxy.
Yet he can use the same tools to inflict the most unbelievable pain on his own
species.
Man may yet destroy all life on this planet.
Green, green earth, would you not be better served without Man?

Chapter Six

A Change in Venue

Water, water, the sweet taste of water. For one brief moment, Menek transcended time and space as he touched the mouth of the life-restoring, water-filled hose. Time stood still for Menek, his attention totally focused on satisfying his body's seemingly unending demand for water. His severely dehydrated body commanded him to "Drink, drink, and drink again!" Gradually his parched, nearly paralyzed lips regained their memory and began once again to form audible, coherent words. And once more his brain reclaimed primary control over his body as he began to survey his new surroundings.

But no sooner was the body hydrated than the stomach rose to be recognized, resuming its long-standing filibuster to be heard, not ignored. The sun did its part too. It helped to intensify the pounding headache that followed his long drink of water.

The new arrivals were promised food as soon as they were organized into manageable groups. Prisoners who could walk were ordered to line up for a count and evaluation. It only took a few seconds for everyone to suddenly focus on the billowing smoke stack inside the camp. Menek's hunger was abruptly silenced when his eyes became fixed on the stack. He began hoping that this camp too had a factory that manufactured rifle shells.

The prisoners were ordered to line up in rows of five. They were marched into the camp through the gate. The whole camp was ringed with a high-voltage electrified barbed wire fence. As they passed the entrance, Menek immediately spotted a crematorium, with its smoke-filled stack, to the right of the marchers. They marched past several piles of bodies that were stacked like chords of wood on the side of the crematorium. To the left was a large

Appelplatz. They advanced past the prison kitchen on the right, and were finally ordered to stop in front of a bathhouse. The directive was then given to strip completely.

Menek's heart began to race. By this time the prisoners were certain that the "bathhouse with showers" meant a gas chamber. While they were still in Skarzysko they had already been clued-in about the gas chambers in Poland, long before they were shipped out to Buchenwald. News from the "outside" was often received from the free Polish workers that came to work in the munitions factory.

Menek reached for his brother's hand and held it tightly as the doors to the bathhouse opened. The naked men were ordered to leave their clothes and step into the shower room. He could now feel the pounding in his chest. Along with the rest of the new intimates in his group, he could not bring himself to step forward. Prisoner inmates who were working in the bathhouse tried to coax and reassure the new arrivals by saying, "Don't be afraid, these are real showers!" They attempted to reassure everyone, promising them that warm showers with real soap awaited them inside. But their efforts were futile. Finally several soldiers lowered their rifles as an SS officer warned that his patience had reached an end.

Menek continued to hold Chamush's hand as the panic-stricken group hesitantly entered the shower room. The ceiling was lined with rows and rows of showerheads. Paralyzing fear gripped each person in that room as the doors were closed shut behind them. Every eye was fixed on the showerheads. Some men were quietly saying their final prayers; others, like Menek, just held their breath. Suddenly the pipes leading to the showerheads began to rattle. And within seconds, water, warm water, began to spew out of the showerheads.

Utter reprieve filled the room. The tension, only moments earlier, gradually melted away. The mood in the shower room was transformed into miraculous relief. Elation and a gradual outbreak of smiles were followed by a complete surrender to this unexpected event. It was the first time in two years that Menek had a bath. He kept repeating to himself and to his brother, "It's not gas, it's really water! It's not gas, it's really water!"

Every man in that group died a little on that day.

After the shower, the new arrivals were marched in a single file to the disinfection stations near the bathhouse. They moved between two rows of prison inmates that were armed with manually operating disinfecting canisters. The disinfectant was liberally applied to every part, every crevice of the body; modesty by then had long been suspended.

For the first time in two years Menek was lice-free. Each man was then handed a pair of striped pants and a jacket. The processing was completed with a haircut down to the scalp. One narrow cropped strip, about an inch wide and a quarter inch high, was left on top of the head. It ran from front to back. It was referred to as *"Lousestrasse,"* lice street. The actual purpose was to brand the prisoner and make him more identifiable if he escaped. Menek's spirits were momentarily lifted, because he was clean and vermin-free; he began to feel like a human being.

After processing, the Skarzysko contingent was marched to the *"Kleinem Lager,"* the Little Camp. This was a small camp within the Large Camp. The Little Camp served as a transitory clearing station for prisoners who were to be shipped off as slave laborers to the many satellite camps of Buchenwald.

The two camps were like two different worlds, separated by a barbed wire fence. The internal prisoner security force manned the entrance gate to the Little Camp. Inmates from the Little Camp could not enter the Large Camp. However, the reverse was possible, if one had special permission. The Little Camp contained hastily erected barracks, generally called blocks, and large tents. They were extremely overcrowded. Hundreds of prisoners were squeezed into a single unit. Even the center aisles of the barracks were filled with emaciated human beings. Dysentery was rampant in the Little Camp. The intertwined smell of urine, excrement, and dead corpses was even more intense than Menek had witnessed in Skarzysko. It was an unnerving introduction to the camp after his clean shower and haircut.

As Menek and his brother walked further down the hill toward the back end of the camp, they saw a couple of sewage canals that terminated into a small human waste lake, a stench-ridden latrine. Walking skeletons, referred to as "Musslemen," were either lying in overcrowded bunks or on the ground, too frail to get up for their rations. They relieved themselves either outside the tents or in their racks. Their demise was no longer in question; it was simply measured in terms of days. Their resting place was a mound of corpses, some of them still moving, stacked in neat rows in the mud.

> In lush meadows He lays me down,
> Beside tranquil waters He leads me. . .

A rain from an earlier night left the unpaved grounds muddy and difficult to navigate. It was in this setting that Menek and his brother finally received their ration of bread and soup. While they were standing and eating, Menek noticed a couple of "better dressed" inmates interviewing the younger men and boys in the newly arrived group. When one of them finally reached the two brothers, it became clear that he was interested in having brutal *Kapos* identified, ones who were particularly cruel to them and their fellow inmates in Skarzysko. Without hesitation Menek and his brother pointed to "Veiter-Da." This was the very same tyrant who delivered a full-fisted blow to his mother's face on the day they arrived in Skarzysko. Not surprisingly, he received most of the votes. A "meeting" was held that night in his honor; Menek and his brother were invited to attend. The next day he was found floating in the pit of the latrine.

Buchenwald was originally erected in 1937 to imprison political opponents to Hitler. Before the war, the prison held several thousand inmates. It contained a moderate contingent of German communists. Some of them had been there since its inception. These German prisoners ran the internal affairs of the camp. They were well organized and acted mostly as liaisons between the Nazis and prison inmates. Most of them were barrack leaders, often referred to as "Block Elders." In the barracks, their word was law. When World War II broke out, the camp began taking in prisoners of war from many countries. The barracks in the Large Camp were filled with prisoner inmates according to nationality. The Block Elder, however, was generally a German political prisoner, and the next in command was the highest-ranking officer in the barrack. The Jews, regardless of country of origin, were placed in Jewish barracks.

The camp was situated in the middle of a forest, near a stone quarry several kilometers from the city of Weimar. Weimar took pride in being the city where Schiller and Goethe, the "Shakespeares" of Germany, produced their greatest literary works. Only one hundred years later, this same city played host to the Buchenwald concentration camp. Weimar would also play host to the Red Cross delegations that visited Buchenwald—however inspection of the condition of Jewish prisoners or their barracks was not on the Red Cross agenda.

The advancing Allied armies late in 1944 forced the Nazis to close many of the camps in the East and ship its slave labor supply to Germany. Many prisoners did not survive the transports, especially those that were on forced death marches. The Little Camp was bulging with new arrivals, almost daily. The able-bodied men were shipped out to the satellite camps for backbreaking work, which ultimately killed many of them. Those who remained in the Little Camp were made to work in the quarry, hauling boulders to the surface.

By the time Menek's transport arrived in Buchenwald, the entire camp was already bulging with a reportedly 50,000 men. There were no women in Buchenwald except for one barrack, a brothel. It contained well-fed women prisoners for the comfort of long incarcerated prisoner officers, those who achieved a "deserving" status for such a perk. Occasionally, Menek saw some of the women sitting outside their barrack on his way to work.

Judge not, lest ye be judged.

Within a few days of their arrival, several Block Elders from the Large Camp came into the Little Camp. They began to pick out some of the smaller boys from the general population. Their purpose was to keep them out of sight in their respective blocks because these boys had a slim chance of survival in the Little Camp. Menek was one of many boys who were selected. A trustworthy Jewish spokesman accompanying the Block Elders assured the boys that the purpose of *this* selection was to *save* lives. These Block Elders—German political prisoners incarcerated since 1937—were determined to save as many young boys as possible. The inmates in the Little Camp were literally dying by the thousands. When Menek protested, saying that he would not go without his brother, one of the Block Elders made it clear, in a very gentle manner, that each Block Elder could only take one boy per block. He assured him that his brother would be assigned to a "safe" Jewish barrack within walking distance of Menek's barrack. He further promised Menek that he would be allowed to visit his brother periodically. "You will be in my block with Russian prisoners, Block #30," he said. "Your brother will be in Block #23, with Jewish prisoners."

As they were leaving the Little Camp, the Block Elder instructed Menek, "From now on, in my barrack, your name will be Willie, and you will immediately sew onto your jacket lapel an "R" patch."

The "R" stood for Russian. Since the camp held prisoners of many countries, each prisoner was required to display a patch indicating the first letter of his country. Except the Jews: regardless of their country of origin, their letter was "J." The Jews received the worst treatment. The Gypsies and the Russians followed, a close second and third.

For Menek, the change from the Little Camp to the Large Camp was like stepping out of hell into heaven. Even the ground was no longer muddy. The barracks were neatly arranged and comparatively clean. There was a clear system of order. Most importantly, there were no corpses on the grounds.

Block #30, the Russian barrack, was clean. It had a washroom with running water, although sometimes the water was turned off. The toilets were indoors and moderately clean. And in the center of the living area was a table with benches and an iron potbelly stove for winter heat. Menek had never seen luxuries like these in a camp. The barrack even had a window and wooden floors.

Thrown in with several hundred Russian prisoners of war, Menek found that he was the only prisoner inmate in Block #30 who could not speak a word of Russian. Though he was fluent in Polish, Yiddish, and German, these languages wouldn't help him here. In this "sink or swim" environment, Menek forced his lips to rapidly embrace the Russian language. Having had an ear for languages—though he could not read or write in any language—he was able within a few short months to become the designated translator for the Russian prisoners.

The Russian POWs were not told about Menek's arrival until he actually walked into the barrack, however they immediately accepted him as a comrade. The barrack operated like a full military unit. A standard chain of command was followed to the letter. Orders given by the Block Elder were transmitted to the senior Russian officer, a Colonel, then to the junior officers, and ultimately to the troops. Menek's chain of command was the Colonel and the Block Elder. The Block Elder made it abundantly clear to Menek that he was to follow only his or the Colonel's orders, no one else's. Menek's assigned work area was the *"Holzhof,"* the wood yard. His job was to cut and stack wood, but he was only to go there when directly ordered by them. His key objective, as outlined by them, was to minimize his visibility. Outside the barrack he was to move quickly and stealthfully, an art that he had already honed well.

A slice of bread and black coffee was given to each prisoner in the morning. There was rarely any stealing of food in this barrack. In the evening it was a slice of bread and soup. In a few rare instances the soup contained small pieces of meat. The food was fairly distributed without any favoritism. Seconds were distributed on a rotational basis. After the evening soup, roll call was called. Roll call meant having to assemble on the *Appelplatz* in neat formation. Each barrack had an assigned place marked by a stone on the "Grinder," their term for the *Appelplatz* or assembly grounds. Only the inmates of the Large Camp were required to assemble. The prisoners were forced to stand for many hours regardless of weather if the count did not tally. One particular winter night, the captives were forced to stand in a cold, wind-driven rain past two in the morning because the count was short by two inmates. A few hours later the prisoners had to line up again for the morning roll call. A count in the Little Camp was unfeasible because the high daily death rate made the count impossible to track.

If the roll call took less then two hours, Menek seized the opportunity to make a short visit to his brother. First he had to get permission from the Block Elder and return to his barrack before camp curfew. His brother did not have the freedom to come to Menek's block.

Sundays were free days, unless the Nazis devised some collective punishment. On those days the prisoners in the Large Camp had an opportunity to relax, to sing, and recite poetry written generally by camp inmates. These were rejuvenating times for Menek. He and his brother learned to recite or sing the songs written by Jewish inmates. Since Menek had not yet learned to read or write, his ears served as transmitters to his memory bank. The songs and poetry spoke of loss, humanity, hope and home.

Meanwhile the misery in the Little Camp continued unabated. Menek frequently walked along the fence separating the two camps. On those occasions

he experienced strong pangs of guilt when he observed the squalor and emaciated skeletal figures on the other side. Even though he was on the better
side, he continually feared that his situation could change overnight. The
threat of death was his constant companion.

Menek listened with scorn when the intellectual, enlightened prisoners
spoke of a future when civilized courts would obtain justice for them. This
was a topic occasionally touched upon in Block #23, his brother's barrack. He
thought of Jacob the Learned and wondered how he would respond to these
arguments. Menek became particularly annoyed with a few of the inmates
who still clung to the belief that God Himself would mete out justice.

In his newly achieved enlightenment, Menek became very vocal and un-
bending in his debates with the older men. When they talked about courts of
justice, he responded: "I will be willing to talk about courts *after* every Nazi
and every collaborator has been obliterated!" His position on God was
equally cynical: "Is this the God who watched my father fall from a bullet,
shot by the beast that He created?" he asked them. "Is this the same God who
guards over the innocent corpses piling up in the Little Camp and in front of
the crematorium day in and day out? No! No! No! Don't speak to me of God!
There is no God! There is no justice! And there is no hereafter! I will forever
honor the memory of the fallen," he told them, "but I will not honor Him!"

Childhood and adolescence for Menek whizzed by at warp speed. At the
age of twelve he was without faith and without hope in the future. He had become an embittered old man. He was sure that his brother was the only family he had left in his world. His mother, he learned, was taken to a concentration camp near Leipzig, Germany. A reliable source reported that the women
in that camp were taken on a death march. Menek tried to envision a future,
if freedom ever came, with just his brother and himself. He found it extremely
difficult to imagine. In some ways, it was easier for him to deal with his immediate surroundings and day-to-day situations. He let himself think only of
the "here" and "now." His experiences, coupled with an innate survival instinct, led him to adopt a personal credo: First, to get his food and eat it
quickly; second, to seal his emotions in a steel vault for later; and third, to be
on constant alert for life-threatening signs. This meant seeking out and sometimes testing potential hiding places. It also meant he had to continually scan
the terrain for changes that might affect on his plans.

When Menek heard the air raid sirens in Buchenwald for the first time, he
jumped for joy. Finally his kind of justice was going to be meted out to the
Germans. He began to feel an exhilarating sense of revenge. The knowledge
that the Germans were about to get what they deserved released long pent-up
emotions in him. He wanted them to suffer. There weren't enough bombs in

the whole world to satisfy Menek's thirst for retribution. He even felt that if he were killed during an air raid, he would be comforted by the knowledge that they too were dying.

The Nazis had turned him into a bloodthirsty animal, craving German blood. He pictured these exemplars of the "Invincible Arian Race" cowering in their cellars, shitting in their pants with fear. Had he been an artist, he would have liked to paint a scene of the inferno they would suffer, framed by images of the innocent souls they murdered. Only after every Nazi bastard and every collaborator had been bombed into oblivion could Menek's rage be stilled. Only then, he felt, would all those slaughtered innocent souls finally rest in peace.

He stood at the window, along with several Russian POWs, admiring the condensation trails created by the Allied aircraft in the beautiful clear blue sky. The sky gradually became pockmarked with antiaircraft flak. Within minutes, the German Air Force sent up their fighter planes to challenge the bombers. Allied fighters soon met them. The dogfights were quite visible to most observers in the barrack, but it was not always possible to distinguish which aircraft to cheer and which to jeer. These were exciting sights at first, but Menek was eager to hear the sounds of exploding bombs in the midst of his German tormentors. His eardrums longed to feel the sound waves generated by falling bombs. He wanted to see and smell their blood.

Menek's heart leapt with joy when he finally heard the whistles of falling bombs cutting through the upper air. His whole body resonated with the reverberations of the exploding bombs. The planes were dropping all sorts of bombs—concussion, which shattered their targets, and incendiary, which ignited on impact. They were falling mostly on the outskirts of the camp, hitting the munitions factory, the German quarters, administrative buildings, and the stone quarry.

Menek's ears cried out for "More! More!" He pictured German SS and their dogs being pulverized by the concussion bombs. The noise, the clatter, the explosions were not loud enough to sate his need for revenge. He wanted the roar to shake the inner core of the earth. He wanted the thunder to be so loud that it would reach the very souls of the departed. "Look! Look!" he cried out to them inwardly, "Your deaths are now being avenged!" Menek wondered if a small ray of justice was at last starting to pierce through the thick black layers of injustice.

The Russian POWs dove for cover as the ear-piercing whistles came closer and closer, but Menek stood glued to the vibrating window as the barrack walls shook with each exploding bomb. A few times they pulled him down and forced him to the floor for his own protection. The whistles and explosions finally became so loud that it was clear the bombs were falling way too close to the prisoners' barracks.

Suddenly the whole barrack shook violently. Everything turned dark for a brief instant. The earsplitting noise momentarily stunned everyone as debris flew in every direction. When the dust began to settle, Menek was lying on the floor, half-conscious and bleeding profusely from his forehead. The blood was literally spurting out of his head.

A Russian soldier lying next to him pulled off his shirt and pressed it forcefully against the open wound. When one shirt became soaked with blood, another soldier volunteered his, and together they half dragged and half carried him to the prison hospital. Menek was dazed as he made his way between the barrack and the infirmary. His earlier joy was dampened as the pain in his head grew stronger. He was becoming weaker with each passing moment, but he forced himself to stay conscious. As they approached the infirmary, Menek could see many wounded prisoner inmates lying on the hospital grounds. Some had their limbs blown off, some were terribly burned; most seemed beyond help.

Menek was taken directly into a treatment room. He was weak and frightened, but thankful for the help of his barrack mates. When the doctor, also a prisoner, finished examining Menek, he simply said: "We don't have anesthesia, so you will have to tolerate the pain while I treat you. I will first clean the wound with alcohol, then I will remove the shrapnel and sew the wound. It is important that you try not to pass out. I will do my best to be fast and gentle."

Menek was grateful to hear these kind, reassuring words. He did not expect to receive such gentle consideration in the midst of all the chaos. It made the extreme pain that was about to follow more bearable.

He braced himself emotionally as two attendants held him down very tightly. The doctor covered Menek's eyes with a cloth and immediately began the procedure. The pain was excruciating. Menek wanted to scream, but an inner voice kept saying, "Hold on! Hold on!" Words of encouragement streamed from the attendants as they held him tightly on the table. From the distance he even heard the supportive voices of his Russian colleagues saying, "You're a brave soldier!" He forced himself to ignore the intense pain. Several times Menek was about to pass out, but the doctor's words echoed in his ears. The procedure seemed to last an eternity. When the doctor assured his patient that he would survive, the pain became a little more endurable. Besides, he had come too far to give up now.

When the operation was over, the surgeon informed Menek that he removed several pieces of shrapnel from his head. One deeply imbedded piece of metal could not be removed because the hospital did not have the necessary equipment. The doctor suggested that it be left alone in the future unless it caused problems. Menek remained in the infirmary for several hours as aides checked on him periodically. His Russian companions stayed with him and kept telling him that he would make a good soldier. Their words and the doctor's compassion gave Menek a long lost sense of inner peace. He no longer felt that he was fighting a battle all alone.

During his short stay in the infirmary, Menek saw hundreds of wounded brought in for treatment. Many were barely clinging to life either from burns or wounds. The loss of limbs was very high. Countless died from a severe loss of blood. The air raid caught many prisoners at their workplace in the factories. The ammunition factories, the quarry, and the surrounding woods all took direct hits. Only two bombs had dropped directly inside the camp.

Block #30 in fact had not been bombed. The potbelly stove that stood in the center of the barrack had just exploded. Menek could not understand how or why the stove would explode. He questioned several Russian soldiers, yet none of the answers seemed to make sense. He even pressed several of the junior officers, but they too gave him vague, ambiguous answers. Finally the Colonel took Menek aside and ordered him never to bring up the subject of the explosion again. He said if asked by anyone about the bandages or how he received the wound to his head, he was to say that a rock from the quarry struck him during the air raid. Although Menek did not understand the reason for this, the Colonel spoke in such a forceful and unambiguous manner that it left no doubt in Menek's mind that any further questions regarding this subject were taboo. Menek was indeed a good soldier; he never spoke about the potbelly stove explosion again.

During the winter that followed Menek worked periodically in the wood yard. On occasion he even saw his brother there. He was generally told during morning roll call, either by the Colonel or the Block Elder, where to go for that day. Sometimes he was ordered to stay completely out of sight. He never told anyone, not even his brother, where his hiding places were. He always made sure to have several alternate hiding options. He also made it a practice to alternate his routes whenever he was sent to work in the wood yard. He applied the same practice when he went to visit his brother.

Unlike the quarry or factory, where treatment of prisoners was brutal and deadly, the work in the wood yard was not hard. It consisted mostly of collecting previously chopped wood and placing it into containers. Sometimes he chopped the wood or trimmed logs. The foreman, a prisoner inmate, was decent and never mistreated anyone. He treated all his fellow prisoners fairly. The internal prisoner security organization, composed of longtime inmates, made sure to weed out bad foremen and informers. Menek considered himself exceptionally lucky to be in the Large Camp. Prisoner inmates elsewhere, like the Little Camp or the stone quarry, were dying from starvation and backbreaking labor daily.

The winter in Buchenwald was very harsh. The barrack was extremely cold. The smaller replacement potbelly stove that was eventually issued to replace the original one provided very little heat. Roll calls in the wind-blown *Appelplatz* became increasingly intolerable. The SS took particular pleasure in holding the inmates at attention in bitter wet weather for hours. Their favorite sport during a freezing wet rain was to give the order, "Caps on" and "Caps off." One particular night, this game continued well past midnight. The man who did not respond to the order in a snappy fashion suffered immediate punishment. Inmates who collapsed from exhaustion were taken away for "special treatment."

The winter also brought a continuous stream of prisoners transported from other concentration camps in the eastern portion of Europe. Most of them were emaciated skeletons barely able to support their own skin-covered bones. Menek saw these wretched souls on his way to see his brother; they generally passed Block #23 when they were being marched from the train depot to the Little Camp. He also saw them when he walked past the outer perimeter of the Little Camp. He was frequently beset with mixed emotions. In one instant, he felt lucky that he was not one of them. But in the next instant, he was beset by pangs of guilt. His experience had taught him to forecast with relatively good accuracy which ones would not survive. Menek, at the age of twelve, had become an expert predictor of imminent demise.

As the winter began to loosen its grip, Buchenwald became a depository for human slaves. At one point Buchenwald held as many as 80,000 inmates. The Little Camp was bursting at the seams. An accurate count of inmates was impossible to maintain because of the high death rate. A slave labor load brought into the camp one day was soon shipped out to satellite camps within a few days—minus the "selected" rejects. The Little Camp had become a virtual turnstile for human cargo. Eventually the overflow and lack of viable transportation produced forced marches.

As the Allies began to tighten the net around the German army, the Little Camp evacuations turned into death marches. Block Elders in the Large Camp began to hide special prisoners who were in transports slated for forced marches. Menek began to notice additional prisoners in his barrack. They did not muster at roll call, nor were they included in any other lists. He knew this was a matter only to be discussed between the Colonel and the Block Elder. He gradually came to recognize that over an eight-year period, since the camp's creation, the prisoner inmate organization did more than maintain the internal order of the camp.

As spring began its approach, the air raid sirens were sounded more frequently. The thuds of falling bombs could be heard in the distance. The nearby city of Weimar and several outlying areas near the camp were bombed. There was an increased frequency of flyovers by low flying American aircraft. The frequency of camp rumors increased proportionately. The most prevalent rumors were about the distances of the advancing Allied armies, particularly the American army. Some had the army several hundred miles away, while others swore it was within earshot of the camp. The experienced Russian soldiers, however, assured Menek that he would be able to hear the rumble of the artillery once the army got within twenty kilometers of the camp. This was solid, reliable information that Menek could authoritatively carry back to his brother and comrades in Block #23.

No sooner did Menek begin to feel a tinge of hope when an ominous rumor began to circulate in the camp. It spread like wild fire. Supposedly reliable sources reported that the German SS command decided to destroy the camp and all its inmates in advance of the American army's arrival. The plan was to obliterate the camp with aerial bombardment, lay mines, or by poisoning the water supply. On several occasions Menek saw his Block Elder huddle with the officers in his barrack. He also saw several of the other Block Elders in hushed meetings.

There was a palpable anxiety that pervaded the entire barrack. A feeling of utter helplessness swept over Menek. To have come this far—from Tarnobrzeg, Koprzywnica, Skarzysko, his battle with typhus, his rescue from the Little Camp—and now to face this possible end seemed to him the epitome of injustice. Every drop of hope was drained out of him. All the positive feelings that had reemerged since his arrival in Block #30 were rapidly fading.

The population in the camp, especially in the Little Camp, was now being rapidly thinned out. Thousands of prisoners were being moved out in great haste. Some by trucks, some by trains, while others on foot. Menek went on repeated inspection missions of all his potential hiding places. He planned to tell his brother, but only at the last minute. The plan was for each of them to hide in separate places. Menek had not forgotten his brother's tendency to talk in his sleep.

Late one afternoon an announcement was made that all Jews were to report to the *Appelplatz* the following morning to be shipped out to another camp. Chamush stole out of his barrack during the night and removed the jacket from a dead Dutch prisoner. He prepared himself to pose as a Dutchman. Menek had prepared to leave his barrack in order to get to Chamush, but the Block Elder would not allow it. He said that it was much too dangerous to be moving about outside the barracks. Nevertheless, Menek sneaked out of the barrack before daybreak, but he was not successful in getting to his brother. A benevolent foreman sent him back to his barrack. Later on, the Block Elder told Menek that his brother was safe.

That very night—though Menek did not know it—the Block Elders in concert with the internal camp security organization advised the Jewish prisoners not to respond to the order to assemble in the morning. They knew that the German guard force was significantly reduced because every available soldier had been sent to fight at the front, and they gambled on the likelihood that the Camp Commandant would not call for reinforcements.

Menek's barrack was located only several hundred feet from the electrified barbed wire fence. The fence encircled the whole camp. The outer side of the fence was lined with watchtowers spaced several hundred feet apart. Two or three SS soldiers with machine guns manned each tower. In between the towers, sentries with automatic rifles continually patrolled the area close to the fence. Any prisoner that came within a few feet of the fence was shot without any warning. This was the permanent scene that Menek saw daily whenever he went into or out of the barrack. He never allowed himself to get any closer than a hundred feet from the fence.

One night the distant rumble of what sounded like thunder wakened Menek out of a deep sleep. It was early April, when rain and thunder might be expected. Several of his barrack mates attributed it to a distant storm. Soon someone remarked that lightning in the sky was nowhere to be seen, though the rumble continued for some time. This could only mean one thing: that the battlefront was getting close to Buchenwald. Excitement suddenly filled the barrack. Everyone was fully awake even though it was still dark outside. The inmates milled around in hushed conversations. The whole spectrum of human emotions filled the dark barrack; elation turned to guarded optimism, followed by fear and a feeling of imminent doom. The question that weighed on everyone's mind was, "Will the German SS destroy the whole camp before the Allies break through?"

April 11, 1945: Daybreak was fast approaching as Menek began considering his options. When he stepped out of the barrack, he noticed the absence of patrolling sentries on the other side of the barbed wire fence. It seemed very abnormal and suspicious to him. His Russian comrades noticed the same peculiar phenomenon, but they were quick to point out that the watchtowers were nonetheless fully manned with SS soldiers with machineguns at the ready. Their nervousness was heightened when roll call was not sounded. Prisoners were not called to go to work. Tensions increased with each tick of the clock as the morning hours crawled along.

Menek requested permission to go to his brother, but the Colonel denied the request. When, after a few minutes, the Colonel moved to the corner of the barrack to huddle with his junior officers, Menek approached the Block

Elder with the same request. He too, however, denied the request without explanation. Orders were given to everyone to stay in the barrack unless specifically instructed otherwise by an officer. The barrack window became crowded with anxious faces.

Menek had ongoing regrets that he had not left the barrack when it was still dark. He also regretted not telling his brother about his secret hiding places. He realized that time too had become his enemy. Chamush had to know about those hiding places if his life was suddenly in imminent danger. Menek was upset with his own poor planning. He could not forgive himself for these blunders. He paced the barrack nervously, as did many others.

After the noon hour, a Russian soldier who was standing at the window announced very nervously to the Colonel that the watchtower nearest the barrack was unmanned. A tense excitement suddenly gripped the whole barrack. The Colonel then ordered one of the soldiers to go out and check the immediate perimeter of the camp. Within minutes another soldier from a different barrack came in to announce that the German SS soldiers had left their posts. He said the camp seemed to be absent of guards.

Several of the Russian soldiers now began pulling out rifles and pistols from the strangest places. Menek stood in utter amazement as he watched one of the soldiers pry open a floorboard and lift out a rifle. He saw another soldier open the potbelly stove, move a few pieces of wood and coals, and take out ammunition—a hand grenade and several handfuls of rifle rounds. Now Menek beamed, finally comprehending the importance of the potbelly stove as he stroked the injury on his forehead.

It gradually became clear to him that every soldier with a weapon had a clear prearranged assignment. Menek watched with awe as the soldiers busied themselves with cleaning and preparing their weapons. A shot rang out as a bullet suddenly grazed Menek's head. A rifle discharged accidentally and almost killed him. Menek ran over to the careless soldier and began screaming at him: "Not now! I cannot die now!" Several barrack mates took Menek in tow and calmed him down.

Word was soon received that the power to the electrified barbed wire fence was turned off. Within minutes an announcement was made that the fence was cut in a couple of places. At that point Menek was told that he could go to his brother. He ran outside, proceeding in the direction of Block #23, but he could not resist the detour to the *Appelplatz*. He had to confirm that German SS soldiers no longer guarded the front gate. His feet could not carry him fast enough. Prisoners were milling around haphazardly; some were in shock, and others just smiled. There was no jumping for joy, no laughter, and no celebration, just emotionally drained scarecrows shuffling along on the cobblestones.

When Menek reached the *Appelplatz* he saw a white flag hanging at the gate entrance. He also noticed that the prisoner internal security force manned the gate. Still he was not quite fully convinced that he was free yet. An unexplainable apprehension still held a tight grip over him. He quickly turned towards his brother's barrack. As he proceeded down the hill he passed the crematorium. This time the bodies were not neatly stacked one on top of the other; the pile up rate was too great. He looked away, because he didn't want to see movement in the piles. It was too painful to think of these wretched souls, coming so close to freedom, only to end up like garbage in a city dump.

The Jewish inmates in Block #23 were in an upbeat mood. The tension that hung over them seemed to have eased. As the American frontline was getting closer to Buchenwald, the Jews had been singled out for death marches and extermination transports. They were only saved by time; the Nazis had run out of time to evacuate them.

Menek was relieved and grateful to see his brother. They stayed in the barrack for a while, but soon became impatient to see what was going on outside. The *Appelplatz* rapidly became the natural gathering place for prison inmates, to hear rumors and exchange information. Menek and Chamush were standing on the Grinder at four that afternoon when the first American military vehicle rolled through the gates and came to a stop in the corner of the *Appelplatz*.

For a brief moment Menek could not move a muscle. He just stood in frozen silence. Survival and freedom had been abstract concepts to him for so long. He had witnessed too much of the systematic slaughter. He saw too much, felt too much, and lost too much to suddenly turn on a switch to instant happiness.

As Menek's eyes drank in the sight of the American soldiers, the reality of freedom began to sink in. He turned to his brother, and without a word they reached for each other and embraced. Then the two brothers began to dance on the cobblestones. Their long, long nightmare was finally over.

Menek and his brother stepped out of the gates of hell.

Chapter Seven

The Circuitous Search

FREEDOM—a concept, a word, an expression so easily spoken but so desperately won. Freedom once denied transforms itself from an abstract concept to a reality. It is a reality forever engrained in the heart and mind of the one set free.

The elusive, almost forgotten concept of liberty rose over the horizon to greet the remnant of Buchenwald. This was not a mere lifting of physical restrictions. It was an abrupt unshackling of chains around the body, the mind, and the spirit. It was a tangible, almost touchable liberty for Menek, which only a few weeks earlier had been a distant fantasy. Even his stomach stilled its perpetual whining in anticipation of feasts about to come.

The internal prisoner administration took over the running of the camp immediately after the first American jeep left the campgrounds and before the arrival of the full American contingent with its administrative staff. It was a period of two to three days in which he witnessed armed inmates mete out justice to the captured Nazi SS murderers. He took pleasure in seeing the invincible Arian torturers beg for mercy with their bloodstained hands raised high up to the sky as they were marched into the camp's interrogating cells. These very same supermen, only hours earlier, stood with their all-powerful weapons, ready to exterminate anyone for the slightest infraction.

Though he had not yet eaten, Menek's stomach filled up on the feedback transmitted by his eyes. It acknowledged the need of its host to satisfy an even greater hunger, a hunger that was cultivated with each passing day in captivity. Menek needed to experience justice and only Menek's justice. Menek craved revenge for all the evils he had seen. He rejected the existence of any other kind of justice. Yet when it was all over, there was no satisfaction, no joy, and no jubilant celebration. Justice was just an illusion. Menek discovered an emptiness in the pit of his heart. Vengeance would not bring back the dead.

Immediately after the prisoner inmates took over all of Buchenwald, they raided the German SS stores and their livestock. The cooks wasted no time in slaughtering a large number of pigs to prepare pork soup. The soup was fatty and loaded with large chunks of pork. For the first time since his imprisonment Menek could have as much soup as he wanted. Many prisoners, including Menek, began devouring the soup. During this feast a frantic announcement was made by the administration to stop eating the soup. When the inmate doctors saw the fattiness in the soup, they became very concerned that the long-denied stomachs would not be able to tolerate the high fat content. Menek got the word as he was finishing the first bowl. But his stomach would not allow him to stop.

The doctors were soon to be proven right. Within an hour Menek began to throw up violently. Like the waves of thunder, the upheavals came one after another. Menek was soon writhing in pain, along with many other inmates in the camp. His system had no more to give up, yet his stomach kept trying to eject every particle. The bouts of vomiting continued throughout the night. There were moments during that long night when Menek wondered if he would survive. By daybreak, however, his system calmed down enough to allow him to sleep through most of his second day of freedom. Hundreds of inmates did in fact die from that soup. It was too much, too soon. What a cruel insult, to die from eating one's first freedom meal! For Menek, it was one more irony of justice.

The second day also brought news that threw Menek into a complete state of panic. When he heard the news over the loudspeaker that President Roosevelt was dead, he automatically assumed that a reversal of fortune was about to begin. Menek knew how to play chess, but he was politically illiterate. Applying the chess analogy, he reasoned that when the king falls, the game is lost. It took several barrack mates to convince him that while it was tragic that Roosevelt was gone, the democratic system in America allowed for an automatic successor. They assured him that the functions of the government and the military would continue uninterrupted. Nevertheless, he forced himself to get up and go out of the barrack to assure himself that the German SS were not coming back. He needed to go to Block #23 to see his brother and get the thoughts of his coreligionists on the issue of Roosevelt's death and how it might affect them.

It took several days before Menek was satisfied with the answers. Only the arrival of a full contingent of American soldiers and administrators helped to reassure him that he had nothing to fear. They also brought the news that the war would be over in a matter of days. However, the high point for Menek was the arrival of an American officer who spoke Yiddish. He was an officer and a chaplain who proudly displayed the Hebrew insignia on his jacket and helmet. At that point, Menek was convinced that all was well.

Menek was reluctant to go to sleep during the first week of liberation. He was afraid that he might wake up only to discover that freedom was but a dream. During the long period of his incarceration, he had dreamt too many times about freedom and family, only to wake up in the midst of the German-made hell. Freedom was such a precious commodity that he wanted to consciously wallow in its delicious warm sunshine twenty-four hours a day.

The city of Weimar was located about ten kilometers from Buchenwald. Menek needed to constantly test and reinforce his freedom, so he hiked into the city on several occasions. Sometimes he was able to hitch rides on American military vehicles. The German civilians were much less accommodating. Immediately after liberation some of the young people in the camp were issued special uniforms that identified them as former prisoners of Buchenwald. Drivers of vehicles acquainted with the Buchenwald-Weimar area immediately knew that Menek was a Buchenwald survivor. Still, he enjoyed the freedom of being able to meander through the streets of Weimar, looking at store windows, gazing at its multi-story buildings, and walking through the city parks. He also enjoyed observing a modicum of normal life, although he was envious when he saw families walking together. Most of the Germans who passed him in the street avoided making eye contact; they gave him a wide berth.

Even though his stomach was finally satisfied and fear for his life removed, he continued to feel the aching absence of family. He and his brother agreed that they needed to embark on a search to find out if anyone in their family was left alive. Menek and his brother were informed that the women from Skarzysko had been taken to a camp near Leipzig. As the Russian front was advancing on Leipzig, the camp was evacuated and its women inmates were forced on a long death march. They were told that only a handful of women survived the march.

Menek had long stopped believing in miracles, yet he and his brother refused to accept the thought that their mother was "no longer here." They swore to each other to leave no stone unturned until they ascertained beyond any doubt the fate of their mother. So when the chaplain urged the boys to stay in Buchenwald, as he was making an effort to have them sent to America, they declined his offer. They also declined an offer to be sent on a *"Kindertransport"* to France or Switzerland. They had made up their minds to head in the direction of Leipzig to find their mother.

Several weeks after liberation, Menek and his brother were attempting to formulate a travel plan when a man came into the barrack and asked for the two brothers. He proceeded to ask them several questions about their mother. At first the boys were frightened, expecting to hear the worst. He quickly assured them that he did not come with bad news. He only wanted to make sure that he was in fact talking to the right brothers. When he was satisfied that he had found them, he pulled out a piece of paper out of his pocket and said, "I have a letter from your mother."

Menek stood motionless, hardly able to breath, as the man handed the letter to his brother. His eyes locked onto his brother's lips as Chamush began to read each word slowly and haltingly. Menek was overwhelmed with uncontrollable envy that his brother was able to read his mother's handwritten words. Up to that point, the news about the women's transport out of Skarzysko was so bad that he would not even allow himself to think about it. As Chamush continued reading the letter aloud, Menek felt terribly cheated that he was unable to decipher his mother's carefully written message himself. When his brother finished the last words, Menek snatched the letter from his hands. He had an irrepressible need to feel the piece of paper that was once held by his mother.

The letter was short, but to the point. She wrote that she and Hanue were alive and that they were staying with a German family in the town of Wurzen. It was difficult for her to come immediately to Buchenwald, she said, but she would attempt to get to them in a few weeks. The letter ended with words of love and encouragement.

That letter was enough to convince the two brothers to waste no time. They immediately prepared to leave Buchenwald and travel in the direction of Wurzen. There was no packing to be done, no ATM machine from which to draw cash; they prepared to leave with just the clothes on their backs and some extra food. A number of well-meaning inmates were unable to persuade them to wait a little longer. The adults argued that most bridges in Germany were destroyed and the railway system was in shambles. Moreover, Wurzen was in the Russian zone and Buchenwald at that time was in the American zone. The Russians allowed entry into their zone, but exits were very difficult. They emphatically warned the boys that once they crossed into the Russian zone, any attempt to return would be virtually impossible.

Victory in Europe had been declared a few weeks earlier; Germany was still in a very chaotic state. Travel in general was ill-advised and considered especially unsafe. However, nothing short of chains would stop the two young brothers from their appointed rounds. They were determined to recover the only known living remnant of their family—their mother and cousin.

On a sunny afternoon late in May, almost a full year since their arrival, Menek and his brother said their good-byes to Buchenwald. Like two hobos, they carried with them a small bag of food, plus the identification cards issued to them by the German-American Administration. They did not look back as they embarked on their journey, so eager were they to experience once again the embrace of their "Momushu."

The hike down the hill towards Weimar was made in silence. Each boy was lost in his own thoughts. Their steps were brisk, filled with a mixture of anticipation and anxiety. Neither signs of spring in the woods on either side of the road, nor the beauty of the rolling meadows below could still the anxiety in Menek's heart.

Wurzen, given the travel routes at that time, was approximately one hundred and fifty kilometers northeast of Weimar. Two factors, however, contributed to a significant increase in the actual travel distance between the two cities. The first was the snake-like boundaries created between the Russian and American forces; the second was the destruction of bridges and railroads during the war. The boys were forced to trek first east to Dresden, and then northwest to Wurzen. Their route would be the equivalent of two long legs of a triangle.

Halfway to Weimar, an American military vehicle stopped to give them a lift into the center of the city. After talking to several people in Weimar about the best available travel options, they walked to the railway station to catch a freight train going east. At the depot a railway worker advised them to wait at a particular track. They waited several hours until the freight train finally arrived.

Menek froze in a panic when he saw a line of empty boxcars. A battle erupted within him—between memories of his last train ride on the one hand, and the promise of a future on the other. A flood of the boxcar images flashed before him, preventing his feet from moving his body forward. Yet the pull of a warm reunion and a mother's embrace predominated and ultimately forced Menek to press ahead. But as soon as he lifted himself into the boxcar he grabbed each door, and with the help of his brother, fiercely shoved it to the maximum open position. Then he picked up some bailing wire that was lying on the floor and doggedly tied the doors into their wide-open positions.

Darkness was approaching by the time the train began to move. Menek and Chamush settled back into a corner of the boxcar. They ate some of their food, chatted a little, and eventually fell asleep. Menek slept very restlessly. He awoke frequently, feeling out of sorts and extremely nervous. The freight train grinded along at a very slow pace and frequently made abrupt stops between stations. Sometimes the stops lasted a long time, which intensified his anxiety.

Menek was worried because he and his brother had no way of communicating with their mother. She had no way of knowing that her boys were on their way to Wurzen. He was afraid she might attempt to travel to Buchenwald while he and Chamush were heading towards Wurzen. The slow crawl of the train added to his worries.

The following day as the sun began to make its presence over the horizon, Menek sat himself down at the open door, allowing his feet to dangle over the side. He looked out over the rolling meadows, reflecting on the train ride only a year earlier. Suddenly he was gripped by an irrepressible desire to yell out loud: "Look, Jacob! Look, Jacob! I can get off this train any time I want! I am free! I am free! I have all the food and all the water I need! No more Skarzysko! No more Buchenwald! I AM FREE!"

He sat at the wide open door for a long time while his brother continued to sleep. Soon the train meandered slowly into the city of Erfurt.

Much to the dismay of the brothers, they found out the whole night's trip was in vain. They had gone in the opposite direction. After a short argument as to whose fault it was, they resumed their journey. Menek was upset because it was the first argument they had since their incarceration in the camps.

Since the train crept at such slow pace, the boys decided to try their luck with hitchhiking and walking. On the second day, they traveled on motorized vehicles and horse-drawn wagons, with lots of hiking in-between. Most of their hiking was on bad roads and over damaged bridges. By nightfall, the two travelers were satisfied that they had made good progress, especially when they were told that the Russian zone was within close reach. Sheer exhaustion finally forced them to seek food and shelter for the night.

They came upon a large farmhouse and asked the farmer if they could sleep the night in his barn. Their food supply was pretty much depleted so the farmer brought out to the barn a meal consisting of bread, cheese and milk. For Menek, it was a feast.

While the boys were eating this meal, the farmer spoke apologetically, insisting that he had nothing to do with the Nazis and claiming ignorance about their atrocities. The farmer initiated this conversation, which the boys were eager to end. This was of course the same story Menek had heard from Germans on his earlier forays into Weimar. He would hear the same excuses and apologies over and over as they trekked across Germany on their circuitous route.

After the meal Menek put his head down on a bed of straw and fell asleep instantly. He slept through the night without ever getting up once. He would have continued in his slumber had the rooster outside not announced the beginning of a new day. He woke up ravenously hungry and wasted no time in helping himself to fresh milk directly from the cow's udder. He then proceeded to the chicken coup where he retrieved a few eggs, punched a small hole in each and successively sucked out its contents.

Chamush soon arose too; he ate some of the food left over from the previous night and without further ado, the two brothers set out in an easterly direction. This was the direction the boys were advised to take. After the first day's fiasco they were sure to check, recheck, and positively confirm the accuracy of their information. Their intermediate destination was Dresden.

The sun was still hiding beyond the horizon as the two brothers began their hike along the side of the road. They periodically came across destroyed German military vehicles; some of them still had the stench of death and war. The fields were lush with nature's beauty—green meadows, fully blossomed trees, birds freely circling overhead in search of their morning feast. Menek once again was lost in his own thoughts. As he observed the sparrows in flight, he asked himself, "Why did birds rarely circle Buchenwald or Skarzysko?"

He already knew the answer: Even the carcass-eating crows were ashamed to partake in such ill-gotten gains.

As the sun rose in the sky, the boys quickened their pace. The dew in the fields evaporated, rushing to join the family of white scattered clouds high up in the sky. Menek and Chamush were also determined to join their family, however small the remnant. The anticipated reunion added fuel to their steps as they burned one kilometer after the other. They tried on several occasions to wave down various vehicles, but without success. The sun too showed little mercy as the noon hour approached, yet neither Menek nor Chamush entertained any thoughts of resting.

As utter exhaustion began to take its toll on them, an American military truck appeared in the distance. The driver recognized the Buchenwald uniforms and stopped without any hesitation. Menek and Chamush were able to communicate to the two American soldiers, with a liberal share of hand motions, the purpose of their mission. During their animated exchange with the boys, the Americans kept asking if they were sure they wanted to cross into the Russian zone. They wanted to make sure the boys understood it was a one-way trip. After the brothers assured them that they were well aware of what they were doing, the soldiers promised to take them as far as the Russian zone, a distance that would have taken more then a day by foot. Menek's grateful smile must have touched the soldiers because after the boys climbed into the back of the truck, the Americans gave them K-rations, water, and two bars of chocolate. Menek was not used to such acts of kindness, particularly with things relating to food. He and his brother expressed their appreciation in a display of animated hand motions and body language that left no doubt about their gratitude. His faith in humanity was gradually beginning to move towards the positive side of the scale.

Menek leaned against the back panel of the truck just as it started to roll. He immediately began eating his K-ration. He and Chamush exchanged pleased smiles. The sun too broke out in a beautiful smile, sending its warm embracing rays over their shirtless bodies. The hum of the truck's engine, combined with the warmth of the sun's rays, lulled them to sleep. Menek fell asleep before he finished eating. So did his brother.

They reached the Russian-American crossing point in the late afternoon. As the boys prepared to disembark, the American soldiers provided them yet with more food—tins of Spam, Carnation Evaporated Milk, baked beans and a box of crackers. Then the soldiers led them over to the American checkpoint. The soldiers wasted no time in explaining to the American officer at the gate the purpose of the brothers' mission. After presenting their documents, Menek and Chamush were allowed to proceed. As they approached the Russian check-point, they turned to wave a final good-bye to the American soldiers. Menek's love and admiration for the American soldier rose exponentially that day.

Menek and Chamush held out their travel documents when they approached the Russian soldiers. Utter surprise, bordering on shock, swept over their faces as Menek began to explain in clear fluent Russian the purpose of their trip. They became a little suspicious when he told them he had spent a year in a Russian barrack at a concentration camp. At first, they didn't believe him. They were only convinced when Menek began singing and reciting some of the Russian patriotic songs of the day. While they were not as accommodating as the Americans, the Russian guards were able to advise them about where to go and the best means of transportation. Having the ability to communicate both in Russian and German gave the young travelers the edge they needed to check and recheck hastily given directions.

Although their strength was rapidly waning, the fear that their mother might start out in the opposite direction gave them the necessary incentive to press on. Before nightfall, they were fortunate enough to find a few more rides. They had to cross several bombed-out bridges that were closed to vehicular traffic on foot.

A clear moon surrounded by an array of brightly studded stars provided light on a quiet road as the boys pushed on late into the night. An occasional rustle from behind the trees interrupted the hypnotic song generated by hundreds of chirping crickets. Sheer exhaustion eventually prevailed over their stubborn will and forced them to stop for a night's rest.

A bombed-out one-story structure at the side of the road became their "hotel" for the night. Menek and his brother settled down in the only corner that was joined by two partially destroyed brick walls. The other two walls lay neatly in a big pile in the center of the bombed structure. Overhead, millions of stars gathered to greet and smile upon the intrepid guests.

The restaurant doors were flung open within minutes of their arrival. The menu had a wide array of choices. They were:

Succulent Spam cut in generous portions.
Hickory-smoked baked beans, arranged in a mouth-watering display.
Delicious squares of gently browned crackers.

Carnation Evaporated Milk, to enhance the palate.

And for the pièce de résistance, the hotel served a delicious bar of American chocolate.

It was a meal fit for kings. As he ate his dinner he was sure that he had gone to heaven. Once again he thought back to the American soldiers, feeling grateful to them for providing such a delicious meal.

The boys were up at the crack of dawn, anxious to meet the day head on. A nervous excitement gave every movement a hurried tenor. There wasn't much conversation between them. They were wrapped up in their own private thoughts. Menek would not allow himself to think of the possibility that on this very day they might finally reach Wurzen to embrace his mother and Hanue. Such thoughts, while pleasant, were also laced with painful negative "what if's"—What if their mother and Hanue had already left Wurzen in the direction of Buchenwald? What if transportation was not as available as the day before? What if a bombed-out bridge would force a day's detour? Chamush must have had similar thoughts, because they simultaneously accelerated their activities.

Rain clouds were beginning to form up ahead as they started their hurried hike out onto the open road. The only sound was the crunching gravel under their feet. A steady light rain began to fall, but they kept pressing forward. Numerous vehicles passed, but none stopped to offer them a ride. They reached the outskirts of a small town by mid-morning, just as their feet were beginning to complain. Menek and Chamush had learned from experience to follow the railroad tracks to get to a town's station, so they turned off the road to follow the tracks. Soon after the rain stopped, the two drenched and tired travelers reached the center of town.

There they stopped numerous people for advice on travel to Wurzen. Some onlookers turned away from the boys because they looked like vagabonds. Of the many suggestions that were given to them, some appeared to be contradictory. One thread seemed to connect most of the advice-givers. It was that two crossings over a small river along the route to Wurzen were destroyed, so trains and trucks could only go so far on either side of the river.

Menek noticed an older man sitting on a bench facing the tracks. He was leaning on a cane, smoking a pipe and listening to all the various advisors. Finally he made a "come here" motion with his right hand. The boys were instantaneously drawn to him. As soon as he uttered the first few words, both Menek and Chamush sensed that he spoke with authority. Each word spoken seemed more like a command than friendly advice. Basically he instructed them to wait for a freight train that was due within the hour. He said the train would take them within several kilometers of the river. They were then to hike across a temporarily erected footbridge and continue walking several more kilometers on the other side until they reached a small railway yard. Freight trains to Wurzen, he assured the boys, ran somewhat regularly from that yard. He said that every train from that point would go by way of Wurzen.

A freight train did in fact arrive within the hour, on a track that was pointing in the direction that the boys were heading. The pipe-smoking man, still sitting on the bench, motioned to the boys to scurry over and jump on to it quickly. They wasted no time; within seconds they were comfortably seated inside an empty cattle car.

Menek's anxiety to get to Wurzen grew in intensity with each minute that the train delayed its departure. He tried to imagine what their reunion would be like. But the constant fear that their mother might be heading in the opposite direction hung over his head like the black clouds that were forming in the distance. The thought of a potentially devastating disappointment was too much for him to bear, so he forced his mind to think of other things.

Menek was grateful when the train finally began to move. Its direction was away from the dark clouds and into warm, clothes-drying sunshine. He removed all his wet clothes and basked in the delightfully hot summer sun. The train's speed lifted his spirits once again.

They arrived at the river crossing in the early afternoon. The steaming hot sun made the subsequent trek to the other side difficult. Nevertheless, the two brothers continued at a sprinter's pace. The extra thrust in their feet came from the sudden realization that they were within a few hours of Wurzen. Their thoughts were focused on just one goal: to get to the railway freight yard as quickly as their feet could carry them. To Menek, the time to get there seemed like an eternity.

At the railway depot the boys spotted several railroad men working on one of the tracks. On another track Menek saw riggers unloading large machinery from a flatbed railway car. None of the freight cars in the multi-rail yard were hitched to an engine, so their hopes of leaving very soon were quickly dashed. The brothers rapidly surveyed their travel options, but the only realistic option remained "travel by rail."

The boys were generally treated with suspicion or incredulity whenever they engaged adults in conversation. It usually took several minutes before most adults accepted the truthfulness of their story. Or they just walked away. Only a few tried to be accommodating. After speaking to most of the workers in the area, the boys were able to learn which train was likely to be leaving next.

The late afternoon brought with it thunder and lightning, still in the distance. It also ushered in a coal-puffing locomotive. The two travelers ran to the flatbed cars as soon as it became evident that an engine was about to be hitched to the cars. Short little Menek had difficulty reaching the step rung, but with his brother's help, he eventually made it.

The flatbed car was long, without sidewalls or a roof. It had only one small front bulkhead. As soon as the train began to move the car became fully "air-conditioned." The two brothers were almost immediately forced to huddle together when a piercing rain, accompanied by heavy thunder and lightning, inundated the train. A spark-spewing, ash-belching locomotive engine added to Menek's extreme discomfort. He was convinced that his body, and particularly his head, acted as a magnet for the flying sparks disgorged from the engine's stack. At one point when the train was going through a large open field, the thunder and lightning were so relentless that Menek began wondering if he would survive the ride. "What a cruel injustice, to die now," he thought.

The storm lasted about fifteen minutes. The rain too departed soon after. Even the wind turned its direction so that the sparks were no longer landing on the heads of its two passengers. As if to announce the dawn of a new day, a beautiful rainbow gradually came into full view. It crowned the lush green meadows beneath the speeding train. Each passing mile brought new beauty to Menek's eyes. Menek related to the pureness of nature uncontaminated by human hands. When the train went past a small forest, he instinctively evaluated its density. The density of a forest, he had learned, determined its quality as a hiding place.

The train's sudden deceleration, accompanied by periodic toots of the whistle, suggested to the boys that they were finally approaching the city of Wurzen. At first Menek observed houses interspersed between farmed fields, but as they got closer to the city center the distances between houses diminished substantially. When the train slowly approached the main station, they lost patience and jumped off before it came to a full stop. The sprint across numerous tracks took a matter of seconds.

The two travelers went into the station washroom to clean up from the trip. Their faces and clothes were covered with soot. It was a very hurried wash. As they were going through this process, it occurred to them that they had no real plan for their search in the city. They agreed to walk out into the city and make verbal inquiries. Since nightfall was soon approaching, the pressure to move quickly mounted with each passing minute.

When the two brothers exited the station, they could not quite decide in which direction to go. A young woman pushing a baby carriage crossed the street, walked straight up to the boys and simply asked, "Are you the Schiller brothers?"

For one long moment Menek forgot to breathe. Chamush, apparently able to recover faster, answered in the affirmative. At that point, she welled up with tears and said, "Come, I will take you to your mother."

For the next five minutes the only sounds that were heard were the squeaking wheels of the baby carriage. Neither Menek nor Chamush were able to formulate any words or questions as they were still trying to recover from shock. The woman too was choked up, unable to talk. When she finally spoke, she said that she promised their mother that one day she was going to bring the boys to her.

This young woman was a member of the family that provided shelter for their mother and Hanue after the two escaped from the death march. A German family—mother, daughter and her husband and a child—literally took their mother and Hanue into their apartment to live with them. The matriarch's husband was imprisoned by the Nazis, accused of being a Communist.

During their walk to her apartment she explained that she often came by the railroad station with the hope of finding the two brothers. But, she added with a smile, she never expected it would be this easy.

"We cannot just walk into the apartment because your mother is not expecting you at all. The shock might be too much for her," she said. Quickly, she formulated a plan: "I will go upstairs to our apartment on the third floor, while you will wait downstairs near the stairwell," she instructed. "At the appropriate time I will bring your mother down to you."

Menek wanted to scream out "walk faster!" but the rambunctious toddler, squirming in his carriage and demanding to walk, had other plans. It was a fifteen-minute walk that seemed like time without an end.

As they entered the apartment building Menek's heart began pounding. He and Chamush stood quietly as the woman knocked on her neighbor's door, to ask her to watch the toddler while she went upstairs. The news spread like wildfire throughout the building. Within seconds neighbors came out of their respective apartments, whispering in hushed tones to one another. The wait was sheer torture for Menek. He was sure that if he waited another minute, his heart would burst out of his chest. Just as he was about to run up the stairs, he heard a scream that penetrated all the walls of the building.

Within a flash, his mother and Hanue were racing down the staircase. He and Chamush rushed upwards, meeting them on the second floor. Their embrace released the floodgates of emotions that seemed buried forever. Menek had not cried since the time in Skarzysko when he begged the SS commander to save her life. Now his long-parched eyes spouted limitless tears. The slow reversal of the process—from "old man" back to boy—began at that moment.

The four windblown stalks stood on the staircase landing, intertwined in each other's arms, unable to release their grip. The emotional release trickled out so slowly that no one could let go for at least thirty minutes. Menek looked up and down at all the neighbors observing the emotional reunion. He was surprised to see tears of sympathy in their eyes. It was the first time he ever saw Germans displaying sympathy for Jews.

When night fell the four survivors found themselves squeezed into one bedroom. Had they been in a mansion containing one hundred rooms, they still would have stayed in one room. No one slept much that first night. When Menek did fall asleep, it was only for very short periods of time. He once again had the heightened need, as on the first few nights after his liberation from Buchenwald, to reassure himself that this was not a dream.

Chapter Eight

A Search for Remnants

Menek basked in the warmth of his newly reunited family. There was lots of hugging and touching in that initial period in Wurzen. Menek needed to frequently reassure himself that the truth he was experiencing was not a dream. Though he enjoyed exploring the city, his need to be within arm's reach of the family was so strong that any exploration without them was out of the question.

On one occasion when Menek took a stroll with his mother, they saw a Russian officer attempting to communicate with a local policeman. It quickly became obvious to all the onlookers that the language barrier was causing a problem. Without missing a beat, Menek stepped forward to provide a quick, uncomplicated translation.

His mother stood there with her mouth wide open in utter amazement. She had heard about his stay in a Russian barrack at Buchenwald, but she had never heard him speak Russian. Menek smiled inwardly when he saw the pleased look on her face as he was relaying the comments back and forth between the Russian officer and German policeman. He recalled her pleased look when she used to watch him ride his father's bicycle around the courtyard garden. He loved seeing that look of pride in her eyes once more.

Gradually Menek's curiosity and desire to explore began to predominate over his fears. In due course, he ventured out into the city all by himself. His expeditions at first were short, but they progressively stretched out in time and distance. His outings soon became a point of contention with his mother. Her natural instinct was to keep her "baby" close to her. However, Menek was no longer a baby, nor a child. He had been ground down and honed into a "survival warrior."

Menek also had an insatiable need to continually test, feel, taste, and experience his freedom. He wanted to see "normal" life in streets and alleyways. He needed his mother's love and attention, but he also longed for something more. He felt an emptiness, a void that had to be filled, yet he could not identify or describe what would fill it. This feeling was particularly intense when he studied the faces of the German people during his ventures out into the city streets, or observed their "whole" families, or saw them walking with their four-legged pets.

Once the struggle for physical survival had abated, he began to feel the loss of the whole family. He secretly hoped he might find his father alive. Often he fantasized that one day he would turn a corner and see his Tatush standing there. He clung to the hope that the news he and Chamush received while still in Skarzysko, that their father was shot, was false—even though two witnesses subsequently corroborated it.

Menek was not a dreamer, nor did he believe anymore in miracles. Yet, when it came to his father, he found it extremely difficult to let him go. He frequently dreamed of him; at night he had visions of Tatush entering the room, hugging his family and bringing lots of presents. With him in their midst, the world seemed right side up again. And so the struggle between pragmatism of an old man and fantasies of a young boy continued to rage in Menek's mind.

Menek was repeatedly angry with himself when he allowed childish, unrealistic thoughts to enter his psyche. He dared not share these feelings with anyone, fearing they would consider him mentally unbalanced. He had seen many men in the camps lose their cerebral balance. Besides, he considered these emotions so private and so raw that he could not tolerate the thought of anyone touching them, or possibly make light of them. Menek buried his secret longings in his personal steel vault.

The family's German hosts in Wurzen were gracious and charitable in allowing them to stay several weeks while they all regained their strength. Still, the need to find family, any family, was uppermost in everyone's mind. The obvious decision, therefore, was to return to Poland.

There were, however, several obstacles that had to be overcome. First, most of the railways were destroyed, but travel by foot, given the distance, was out of the question. Second, passenger trains, though few and far between, were also out of the question because they had no money to buy tickets. Third, the border crossing between Germany and Poland would be very difficult because the Russians were exceptionally careful not to allow German Nazis any escape routes.

One advantage the family had was the ability to speak several languages. Menek's mother had a thorough education in German literature and was flawlessly fluent in German. She was, of course, fluent in Polish as well. And Menek was fluent in the Russian language.

The documents issued to Menek and Chamush before leaving Buchenwald were written in German and English. The papers issued to their mother and Hanue were written in German. Yet explanations at the various checkpoints had to be given in plainly spoken Russian, German, or Polish, depending on the location. Their ability to communicate the purpose and direction of their travel in the required language greatly facilitated their movement across checkpoints.

The departure from Wurzen started on a positive note. After heartfelt expressions of deepest gratitude to their host family, Menek, Chamush, their mother and Hanue began the long journey east, back to Poland.

It was at the height of summer, 1945. The skies were a clear deep blue. The sun radiated on their hopeful faces. Chirping birds provided a melodious song as the four travelers headed towards the train station accompanied by their hosts.

They were able to secure seats on a half-empty passenger train heading east, via Dresden. Their destination was Krakow, the nearest major city to Tarnobrzeg. Krakow was the most likely gathering place for Jewish survivors who once lived in the southeastern corner of Poland. They could use the city as a base while they searched for family in the surrounding towns and villages.

Considering his luck in finding his mother and Hanue, Menek was now buoyed with positive thoughts of finding other family members, and so he eagerly welcomed the trip back to Poland. He began the journey with great anticipation, hope in his heart, and spirit in his stride.

On the train he began to envision the welcome they might receive. Here was a family remnant, he thought, that crawled out of the ashes from an inferno. Surely, after what they had suffered, their old Polish neighbors would open their doors, their arms, and their hearts to welcome them back.

Menek visualized coming back to Poland as "Home, Sweet Home." He longed for the warmth of his own bed, the smell of the house, the never-forgotten courtyard. He yearned to submerge himself in the aroma of the courtyard garden with its beautiful sunflowers at the center. He even hoped he might still find Sahnek, his dog.

He gathered about him all his memories of Tarnobrzeg. These memories sustained him during the darkest hours, not allowing despair to be victorious. Now he needed to walk the streets of Tarnobrzeg, to feel the cobblestones once again under his feet. He imagined himself circling the marketplace on his bicycle and watching his mother shop for provisions for the week.

Menek looked out the window of the rumbling train. This time he sat comfortably erect in his seat, neither hungry nor thirsty. His eyes scanned to and fro, admiring the lush green fields and meadows. The fields were rich with nature's bounty. He marveled at the abundant variety of fresh produce as the train rolled passed apple trees and pear trees just as they were coming into bloom. How beautiful the world appeared to be, he thought. He glanced over to inspect his newly found family, just to reassure himself for the hundredth time, as his mind reflected back to last summer's train ride to Buchenwald. The "old man" within him reared his unwelcome head yet again.

As soon as they departed Wurzen, they officially entered into the world of DPs, "Displaced Persons"—a label yet unknown to Menek that would eventually wreak havoc with his emotions.

The DP, Menek would soon discover, lived in a state of non-existence. He was penniless, homeless and stateless. The very ground he walked on seemed to constantly crumble beneath his feet. His mere existence among the local populace was regarded as a nuisance at best. Compassionate embraces were replaced by cold rebuffs. His gaunt, bundle-toting appearance unmistakably announced his homeless status, even to the amateur spectator.

The sign at the train station read: Dresden. That was the last stop on the comfortable passenger train. Dresden was the last major city they would encounter in Germany, approximately 100 kilometers from the Polish border. This train could go no further. The four travelers needed to hike across the city to a satellite station to continue on their journey. The hike took about two hours, but the long trek did not tire Menek.

He and his brother had been through that city a few weeks earlier, on their way to Wurzen. The metropolis had been bombed into oblivion. There was not one single building left standing intact. This time, during his second tour, Menek saw many more rubble-cleared streets that were made passable for traffic. The only visible means of travel was either by military vehicles, horse-drawn wagons, or foot traffic. Some of the half-standing buildings were appropriated by the military for their headquarters. Seeing the ruins of this city filled Menek with vengeful satisfaction on his way out of Germany.

A train going east was pulling out of the railroad station just as they were approaching the terminal. Menek and his brother, by now seasoned hobos, took this disappointment in stride, but their mother was visibly upset. Her concern was that her two children might have to sleep outdoors that night. Menek and Chamush exchanged amused glances, but said nothing to her. They both realized that she needed to be given the room to be "the protective mother" again. In fact, her frustration served to give everyone a feeling of being an interdependent family once again.

Late that night a long freight train pulling liquid chemical tankers rolled into the station. Each car was equipped with a small lookout compartment at its outer end. Russian soldiers armed with submachine guns were stationed in some of those compartments, but most of the compartments were empty.

Menek found out very quickly from listening to the soldiers that this train was going to Russia via Poland. While the soldiers took a long break inside the station, the family sneaked into one of the unmanned compartments. They stayed hidden until the train began to move eastward.

The train made several stops along the way. Because it was guarded by Russian soldiers, the stops and subsequent inspections were quite short. Periodically one or two soldiers would disembark either to relieve themselves or to inspect the train. It was during one of those stops, at the border between Germany and Poland, that a soldier discovered the two women and the two boys.

Just as he was about to sound the alarm to his fellow soldiers, Menek began speaking to him very rapidly in Russian. The soldier was momentarily thrown off guard when he heard Menek speak in fluent Russian. He stood there, completely baffled, as Menek explained where and how he learned to speak Russian.

Menek knew that he had to speak quickly in order to explain the purpose of their journey. He also wasted no time in telling him that even if a passenger train were available, it would be out of the question for them because they had no money. The soldier asked a few probing questions to check the veracity of his story, but what finally won him over was Menek's recitation of a song the Russian soldiers used to sing during the war. That seemed to authenticate his story. Finally the soldier softened his stiff posture and said, "You can stay, but you will have to be quiet and keep out of sight!"

Everyone breathed a sigh of relief when the train began to roll again. The monotonous click, click, click of the iron wheels on the steel track, combined with the very late hour, forced sleep on the exhausted travelers. But the sleep was to be very short lived. At the very next stop, the soldier came to visit.

The "compassionate" soldier had come to make sure that the ladies were well looked after. As the train picked up speed again, he began pawing at Menek's mother. He had first attempted to make his way to Hanue, but she was successful in parrying his advances. Chamush was fast asleep. This battle went on for quite a while. Finally Menek yelled at him, "Leave my mother alone!"

Just then, the train began to slow down again and ultimately came to a full stop. Rather than deal with the unruly soldier, the four tired passengers disembarked to await another train.

The Russian soldiers imprisoned in Buchenwald were significantly different from those that Menek came to know after entering the Russian zone immediately after the war. Imprisonment, torture, and the constant fear of imminent death created a commonality among the men that allowed their humanity to come to the surface. It forced them to re-evaluate modes of behavior in a world filled with cruelty. Menek also suspected that living with their officers in close quarters had a moderating effect.

Not so outside of the camp. Many of the conquering, machine gun-toting Russian soldiers were unruly and undisciplined, behaving only when officers were present. Unlike the American soldiers, they paid little attention to law and order and showed little compassion for DPs.

Menek's positive feeling at the start of the trip from Wurzen was rapidly beginning to fade.

Chapter Nine

Where Shall I Go?

Krakow, the center of a vibrant Jewish community in southeastern Poland before the war, was now a gathering place for a decimated remnant. For hundreds of years, Jewish life had flourished and multifaceted studies in the Talmud, Yiddish literature, poetry and music flowed like the voluminous waters of the Visla River. But by the war's end, all of that was gone. Gone like a puff of smoke. An eerie silence descended to fill the void that was once an effervescent Jewish community.

Immediately after the war, a small trickle of broken, shock-worn family seekers found its way back to Krakow. They came to pick up pieces. They came in search of something, anything—tangible or intangible. They all sought to recover something of their former lives. Repeatedly the same words were heard from the mouths of survivors:

"Does anybody know of any survivors from my town?"
"Does anyone know about the fate of my family?"
"My name is . . . and I am from. . . . Has anyone come across any of my family members?"

Menek's uppermost thoughts were of Tarnobrzeg—his house, his courtyard, his room. He was looking forward to reunions with family members and neighbors. The young boy in him would not allow him to grasp the magnitude of the tragedy that befell them. He saw many survivors, hundreds upon hundreds. He was therefore buoyed with hope of finding family and friends. He hoped that his dog Sahnek would be there to greet him.

Jews were returning from concentration camps, from hiding places, from the partisans, even from Siberia. A makeshift gathering center for Jewish DPs played host to a flow of transient, shuffling survivors who were continually arriving from or departing to the surrounding towns and villages. Everyone was in search of family survivors; therefore, registering at a central clearing place was crucial. Every survivor made sure to register—giving their name, city of origin, and the names of family members that they were seeking. At the same time, they anxiously scanned the survivors' roster for familiar names.

The DPs were crowded into a multi-story building. Members of HIAS, the Hebrew Immigration Aid Society, ran the center. Hundreds of people were squeezed into the building. Each floor was filled with mattresses neatly arranged in long rows interspersed by small access aisles.

Some of the arrivals were so shell-shocked that all they wanted was to drift back to their homes, hoping to find family members waiting for them there. Still others were merely attempting to recover a few material goods left behind, until they figured out where they were going next. Many were so shattered at the realization of their loss that they could not face a future at all.

Menek's mother and Hanue, after much debate, agreed on a plan of their own. Hanue was to travel alone to Tarnobrzeg, while Chamush and Menek would remain with their mother in Krakow. Hanue, a young woman of twenty, could travel more efficiently alone between Krakow and Tarnobrzeg. She could make inquiries about family members and ascertain the status of hastily left-behind items that would facilitate travel for the four of them.

Menek's disappointment in not being able to immediately travel to Tarnobrzeg was inconsolable. The extended delay was a serious blow to his earlier optimism. He so desperately wanted to return, to walk the streets of Tarnobrzeg, to see his courtyard and the marketplace. All he wanted was to relive one hour of that paradise that was his former home, to touch the memories that had kept him going during all those cold nights behind barbed wire. Now he would have to wait with his mother in Krakow for Hanue's report.

Travel in war-torn Poland was dangerous, especially for Jews. Still Menek could not believe the acts of overt anti-Semitism that were being reported daily. He remembered experiencing occasional sneers and jeers when he strolled on the streets of Tarnobrzeg with his mother or father before the war. But after the war? After the hell that the Jews had been through? He could not and would not accept these rumors as truth. Sneers and jeers maybe, but certainly not the violence that was being reported with increasing frequency. One day before Hanue was about to embark on her trip to Tarnobrzeg, news of the murder of two Jewish men was received. The two men had gone back to their village near Tarnobrzeg in search of family and material goods. They were found slaughtered and dumped in a ditch near the village. That was enough to cancel Hanue's trip.

Thugs and hoodlums were coming out of the woodwork like rats out of holes to feed on the skeletal remains of survivors. Their slander, jeers, and catcalls went unabated in the presence of the policemen. Former neighbors feared returning Jews would reclaim their houses and property. "Go back to Palestine!" was their often repeated taunt. The small number of emotionally and physically exhausted survivors that returned in search of family found themselves once again in fear for their lives.

Poland, a country that was home to over three million Jews before the war, became a hostile landscape to the returning few who survived the Nazi slaughter. Everywhere they heard the cry: "Go back to Palestine!" But even more disturbing was the deafening silence of the genteel Polish population.

Jewish organizational leaders were issuing warnings to stay off the Krakow side streets at night. They also put out strong advisories against travel to the surrounding towns.

Menek's disappointment quickly turned to anger. The beautiful memories of home, juxtaposed against the events that were taking place now, began to torment him. The euphoria of "going home" was rapidly evaporating.

The *coup de grâce* came when Menek personally witnessed a pogrom in the center of Krakow, the enlightened city. Men armed with sticks and knives pounced on survivors, sending many to the hospital. The mayhem spread like a wildfire. It was particularly terrifying because the police did little or nothing to stop the rampage. It only came to a halt after Russian soldiers were called in to restore order. This jolting event set off shudders among the survivors. Menek's feeling of utter helplessness was only matched by the rage that began to build up inside him. His anger at the Polish populace now surpassed his hatred for the Nazis. Still, he was perplexed. "They too suffered at the Nazi hands," he reasoned. "so how could they be so lacking in compassion? How could they be so utterly cruel?" Just as Menek could not wait to reach Poland when he left Wurzen a few weeks earlier, now he could not wait to leave Poland. He even lost the desire to see Tarnobrzeg.

The administrative leaders carried on non-stop meetings, attempting to develop various options in response to the developing events. The returnees from hell huddled inside their building, while two Russian soldiers patrolled the entrance to the building.

It was a hot August night. All the windows were wide open as the DPs settled down on their respective mattresses. Voices and traffic from the street below were clearly heard.

Menek could not sleep. As the still of the night replaced the clamor of city life, Menek heard several Russian soldiers asking their comrades whom they were protecting in the building. The reply that one of them gave shook Menek to the core. He said, "I am guarding a bunch of kikes." The boy hid his face in his hands, as the bitter old man within him resurfaced.

Soon the cry of "Let's go to the Land of Israel" began to swell among many survivors. The old man in him joined in the chorus; he would not allow the boy to be heard. In one short stroke, the urge to return to Tarnobrzeg had vanished.

Motek, a young man who had known Hanue before the camps, began to court her in Krakow. He cared for her deeply and soon proposed marriage. Even though the times were turbulent and the outlook uncertain, he felt that their future together as a married couple held out a promise of normalcy. At first Hanue was reluctant, but Menek's mother, acting as family matriarch, fully supported the union and encouraged Hanue to start a new life with Motek.

Meanwhile, the threesome—Menek, Chamush and their mother—joined a small cluster of DPs that were hastily organized by members of the Jewish Agency to escape Poland's pogroms. The clusters were in effect small manageable contingents of a larger group that was to leave Poland. Their ultimate destination was "the Land of Israel." Hanue stayed behind awaiting Motek's return from a trip that he had taken out of Krakow. After his return, the two traveled to Germany where they were married.

The first leg of the family's journey from Poland to the Land of Israel was via Czechoslovakia. While there is safety in numbers, the trip was nevertheless dangerous and fraught with fear. The British had closed off Palestine as a haven for the Jewish survivors, therefore the actual destination for the DPs had to be kept secret. They had to say they were traveling to Greece, Italy, or somewhere else. The DPs were frequently instructed to give different destinations at border crossings or checkpoints.

A Yiddish song frequently heard amongst the refugees at the time fully and absolutely described Menek's circumstances. Only one who has truly been a homeless fleeing refugee can grasp the full impact of its words:

> Tell me, where shall I go?
> There's no place I can see.
> Where to go, where to go?
> Every door is closed for me.
>
> To the left, to the right,
> It's the same in every land.
> There's no place I can go,
> And it's me who should know.
> Won't you please understand?

The words tormented Menek as he grasped their full meaning and hardened his resolve to leave Poland.

The greatest insult unfolded near the Czechoslovakian border. A Polish border crossing official would not allow passage out of Poland unless he was given some sort of bribe, money or valuables.

Menek's mother had been able to cling to her gold wedding band throughout the war and during her imprisonment, even at times of great personal risk. It was the one thing that the Nazis had not succeeded in taking from her. After liberation she stoically replaced the ring on her finger.

When she approached the border crossing official who blocked their passage and demanded money, she told him they had nothing and pleaded with him to let her and her two boys pass. He was unmoved.

"You are trying to leave Poland?" he sneered. "What's the matter, isn't Poland good enough for you?" As he said those words, he spotted the wedding band on her finger. He pointed to it and said that the three of them could pass only if she gave up the ring. Once again he was unmoved as she attempted to explain the emotional significance of her wedding band.

Menek's blood reached a boiling point as she took off the ring and placed it on the table. At that moment, he felt he was capable of committing murder. Had the odds been more even, he would have allowed his anger to rule. But instead he had to bury his fury in his emotional vault. Again he wondered if there was such a thing as justice in the world.

The tension was considerably eased as soon as the DPs crossed into Czechoslovakian territory. While not welcomed with open arms, Menek no longer felt the hostility that was so palpable in Poland. Group leaders from the Jewish Agency had arranged travel, meals, and sleeping quarters for them. Prior to their departure from Poland each person was given a rucksack with the barest essentials. Although ample portions of food were distributed at each meal, hoarding was still commonplace. For survivors, food remained the most precious commodity for a long time. Menek continued to rest his head on his rucksack at night, to protect the stashes of food within it.

Their trip through Czechoslovakia was relatively brief. The weather, the landscape, and the citizens provided a warm, calming atmosphere. Menek began to gradually shed the bitterness he had accrued in Poland. Unlike his brother or others his age, he became a slave to the "news." He had an intense interest in world events, especially those that might impact on his life. Since he could not read or write, he relied on radio and word of mouth reports. While spending some time in Prague and Bratislava, Menek was able to experience some degree of normalcy. He was given the opportunity to visit famous historical city landmarks. Until that time, life for Menek was primarily a day-to-day affair. The idea of going back in time to learn about earlier generations never entered his consciousness before. Once again, he was frustrated by his illiteracy. "So much to learn," he thought, "but in what language?"

The vogue among the DPs during that period was to learn and practice Hebrew. Various lectures and classes were also given on kibbutz life, agriculture, and self- defense, in preparation for their lives in Israel.

Meanwhile, the constant search for family members never stopped. It was like a thread woven through every activity, every conversation, and every gathering. A person holding up a sign with the names of missing family members was a commonplace sight. Heartbreaking cries followed after bad news, and on rarer occasions, tears of joy at news of possible reunions.

Menek the boy kept hoping that sooner or later the clinging threesome might celebrate the discovery of a family survivor. It was almost a reflex to begin a conversation with a stranger by giving one's name, city of origin, and the names of missing family members. As long as one kept searching, one did not have to face the reality of a decimated family. The acceptance of the enormity of loss could be delayed so long as one kept on searching for survivors. For many, the search allowed them to live in a state of denial.

Menek the old man, despondent and depressed, gave up hope and the desire to search. The most recent events in particular, coupled with his experience in the war and the camps, drove a wedge between the old man and the boy, creating an emotional chasm that became impossible to bridge. Neither the boy nor the old man was capable of articulating his innermost feelings. To make matters worse, his mother and other adults paid little attention to his emotional baggage, which they did not consider comparable to the losses they had suffered or the trials they still faced. Besides, they reasoned, as a child he would soon overcome his experiences. So once again he was forced to bury his unvented pain.

Though their stay in Czechoslovakia was relatively brief—only a few weeks—their journey through Austria was even briefer. The legion of refugees grew with every stop along the way. By the time the multitude reached Germany, they were counted in the many hundreds. "How strange to be back in Germany after all this wandering," thought Menek. This time he found himself in the city of Wells, in a large DP camp established by UNRRA, the United Nations Relief and Rehabilitation Agency. It was basically a tent city, hastily erected to accommodate homeless, fleeing Jews on their way to the Land of Israel.

The camp was largely administered by the JWB, the Jewish Welfare Board, which played a significant role in the day-to-day operations of the camp. The administrators made every attempt to improve the physical and spiritual life of the DPs. They tried to address the needs of the individual as well as the needs of specific groups. For example, they provided the means to perform an occasional wedding and procured the necessary items to establish a synagogue, such as prayer books, Torah scrolls, and the like.

Weddings were such welcome events that the whole camp was generally invited. Each and every wedding ceremony included lengthy prayers for departed parents, brothers, and sisters who could not take their place under the canopy. There was not a dry eye to be found when the prayer for the departed souls was uttered. It was as though the floodgates of suppressed tears were suddenly flung wide open.

Menek was pleased to attend, closely observe, and indeed take part in these weddings, which generally took place under the stars. However, he never attended any synagogue services. His refusal to do so ultimately became a point of contention between him and his mother.

His mother had been steeped in an unshakable faith in God, a faith that taught her never to question God's omnipotence. This faith carried her through the worst of times and, according to her, was borne out when she was miraculously reunited with her children. But Menek could not reconcile with God. At times he even felt contempt for those who clung to religion. He knew that he was hurting his mother when he spoke or acted negatively with respect to religion and deeply regretted when he added to her pain. And so Menek resolved to stop arguing with her and respectfully go along with the religious observances of his mother. She knew how he felt about these things, but nevertheless it made her happy.

The falling leaves in the Wells DP camp signaled the approach of winter. Some of the facilities were not properly suited for winter weather and the UNRRA administrators were pressed to evacuate many refugees. Those survivors deemed to be in need of physical rehabilitation were shipped to Badgastein, a mountain resort town located near Salzburg in the Austrian Alps. Menek, his mother, and brother were part of that transport. They traveled in a long convoy of American troop transport trucks that rumbled from Germany into the Austrian Alps, much to Menek's enjoyment. He always felt safe in the care of American personnel.

In Badgastein, the DPs were housed in the town's resort hotels. Menek's hotel, Hotel Austria, was located near a beautiful waterfall, another unexpected perk for his morale. The hotel rooms were furnished with several hastily erected two-tier bunk beds. Each room held approximately eight people. Privacy was generally achieved with an artful display of blankets or sheets draped between the bunk beds. These curtains were generally hung at night, but in the daytime they were gone. The accommodations, compared to their earlier experiences, were considered quite airy and luxurious.

The clean, crisp air of the high elevation gave him an exhilarating sensation even when just walking out into the street. The breathtaking snowcapped mountains, the large and small waterfalls, the narrow meandering roadways up and down the mountainsides created a sense of seclusion from the rest of the world. It was a feeling of inner peace rarely experienced by Menek. He often enjoyed hiking, all by himself, just to absorb this new-found beauty.

Winter announced its early arrival with a heavy deposit of snow. Now Badgastein became a winter wonderland equal to none. Mother Nature bedecked herself in her purest white-on-white finery. Even the waterfall next to his hotel modified its constant roar to a subdued hush. The winding roads around the mountainsides disappeared under nature's white quilt. Menek had never experienced such beauty. For the first time since his liberation from Buchenwald, a complete relaxation washed over his body. Bitterness, his constant companion, began to fade into the background. Skiing, sledding, mountain climbing, and carefree play began to take center stage.

Life in Badgastein eventually took on a somewhat normal routine. Menek was thrilled to finally begin school. Three classrooms were hastily arranged to accommodate a very small number of students. The administration was anxious to establish some degree of normalcy, even though the length of the DPs stay in Badgastein was uncertain. Menek even began taking piano lessons.

The lessons in the school were given in Hebrew because everyone expected to eventually go to Israel. Kibbutz life and lessons in agriculture were part of their curriculum. Even though learning to till the soil was given top billing, Menek was anxious to learn to read and write as quickly as possible, before another war befell them. He had always been envious of his brother's ability to read and write in Polish. Since his shocking post-war experiences in Poland, his desire to learn to read and write in Polish turned into contempt for that language. He even stopped conversing in Polish. He felt most comfortable speaking Yiddish.

His favorite after school activity, particularly in the winter, was skiing. He and several other boys formed a clique of friends that skied together after school. The ages of the boys in the group ran between twelve and seventeen. Since similar age groups were at a high premium, age differences were virtually unnoticed. By the time spring began to show its early signs, Menek had become a very proficient skier. He was even able to make several respectable jumps. Those jumps of course, came after numerous black and blue marks on areas of the body one does not mention. The expression, "No pain, no gain," certainly played itself out for Menek on those Austrian Alps. But he also learned the hard way that winter that sled-jumping was not a very smart idea. In this case he embarrassingly concluded, "No gain and no brain!"

Winter grudgingly gave way to spring. The milder temperatures washed the stubborn snows from the hillsides and once again exposed the meandering roads. The decibel level of the waterfall's roar rose significantly as the melting snow added to voluminous flow of mountain water. And ice-skating in the ponds below gave way to fishing.

By the time spring established its presence, a number of DPs had left Badgastein for various places in the world. Some families in far-off countries had made the necessary arrangements to embrace their surviving relatives and bring them into their own midst. Some DPs, after regaining their balance, chose to leave Badgastein on their own, either illegally sneaking across the mountains into Italy and ultimately into the Land of Israel, or go elsewhere in the world. Those that chose not to go to Israel were considered unpatriotic and wanting in spirit.

Menek and his immediate family continued their anxious wait for word that they would soon be on the next contingent to leave for the Land of Israel. He conjured up all sorts of visions about his life there. His favorite picture was seeing himself tilling the land during the day and at night, while standing guard, enjoying the juices from all the fruits that the soil produced. He was convinced that only there, in his own land, could he stand tall with his head held high.

Chapter Ten

A Crack in the Door

Menek's mother came from a family of many close siblings. They were four brothers and three sisters. One brother died before the war. In Badgastein she learned that her two sisters had perished in the gas chambers. Three brothers, however, managed to immigrate to the United States before the onset of World War II. She had a vague idea that her brothers lived somewhere in New York, but having been unable to return to her hometown to retrieve letters and documents, she did not have their addresses. At the war's end, she did not have the emotional strength to go through the tedious effort of locating them. She did make several attempts to find them, but always came up empty. What she did not know was that her brothers, with the help of various organizations in the United States, were scouring all available lists of survivors as soon as that information reached their side of the Atlantic Ocean.

Meanwhile, Menek's mother was given notice by a member of the Jewish Agency that she and her two boys were scheduled to leave on the next transport destined for Israel. Such a notice was generally given two to three weeks before the actual departure. Details were deliberately not given because movements to Palestine under the British Mandate required a clandestine cover, due to their blockade of Jewish immigration.

Menek's exhilaration knew no bounds at the receipt of this news. In the months leading up to this notice, Menek had been studying all about Israel and the life of the *"chalutz,"* the pioneer. He studied Hebrew, Middle East history and geography. Thus he gradually developed a love for the land, a land he could call his own. He eagerly looked forward to the day when he could reach its shores.

Menek went into a heady spin that grew in intensity with each day that came closer to their expected date of departure. He could not contain himself, nor could he refrain from sharing the news with his friends, even though he was supposed to be discreet about it. Though he was well aware that the future was still uncertain, this thirteen-year-old gave himself over to an unabashed exuberance. The arrival of spring and the sweet aroma of Badgastein's lilac bushes, his favorite flower, were no match for the joy he felt in finally being able to envision a promising future. He practically floated above the streets of Badgastein. At long last, he was going to the Promised Land.

Menek threw off all his inhibitions; he sang, he danced, and talked with great enthusiasm and animation. His gregarious nature resurfaced, revealing his most affable side and willingness to take center stage. But emotionally, he was never frivolous. His playful side was overshadowed by a seriousness borne of necessity during the war and clearly noticeable by others. This was evident in his attitude towards food, which he still felt compelled to hoard and guard.

Two weeks later, just as they were making preparations for their departure from Badgastein, Menek's mother received a telegram from America. It was short and to the point. It read: "Do not leave Badgastein. . . . Stay where you are. . . . We are sending papers to bring you and the boys to America." The telegram was signed by one of her brothers.

While his mother was euphoric at this new development, Menek found himself on an emotional roller coaster. He was excited by the idea of having more family members that he could claim as his own, but the thought of having to abandon their plans to go to Israel put him into a quandary. First, he was all fired up about going to his own land and working the soil to bring forth fruit from an arid desert. Second, he felt he was going to take part in rebuilding a land that needed him; a land in which he could hold his head up high as a Jew; a land in which he would never again have to endure religious prejudice. For months he had been swept up by the patriotic zeal of immigrating to Israel. He even spoke with distaste about those who chose other destinations, while he lavished words of praise on those courageous pioneers who, in spite of all obstacles, pressed ahead to make a life for themselves in the Land of Israel.

If he agreed to go to America, he would betray himself, as well as his newly acquired friends who shared his enthusiasm. The prospect of going to America made him feel like a turncoat. He was particularly upset when he thought about eventually having to face his friends with the news of their change in plans. Still, he didn't blame his mother for her choice; when his uncles from America threw a life preserver to their only surviving sister, how could he expect her not to seize it? For one brief moment, the budding pioneer in him urged him not to trade Israel for America. But after all his family had gone through to find each other, how could he even consider breaking up this tiny family unit? In the end, his adult pragmatic nature took precedence over the adventurous, idealistic dreamer. Sorely disappointed, the never-to-be *chalutz* reluctantly threw his support behind the move to America.

Suddenly Menek had to change gears. The first thing he had to do was mend some fences with his friends. He started by revising his position on people going to America, verbally showing more tolerance for their choice. In truth, after having had so many pleasant experiences with American civilians and American soldiers, he could think of no better place to live than in the land whose "streets were paved with gold." No matter where he found himself in Europe, sooner or later he experienced various degrees of prejudice. But from the very day that he was liberated from Buchenwald until this juncture in Badgastein, Menek never experienced anything but positive acts from all the Americans that he encountered. Within a week, Menek found he could make the emotional transition from one destination to the other.

Menek's new destination—America!—now rapidly invaded his consciousness. He thought about it every waking hour; he even dreamed about it in his sleep. His anticipation grew to impatience by the time Badgastein's spring foliage gave way to summer's flowers. His focus on learning a new language changed from Hebrew to English. He began paying closer attention to the conversations of American soldiers and picking up phrases. He also began chewing gum more frequently and saving the used piece behind his ear, unless he happened to have a spare strip in his pocket.

He also began to take an interest in the geographical locations of American cities. He wanted to learn all that was "American." He also wanted to know everything about New York City. Menek tried to visualize the building that had more than one hundred stories and whose top floors were hidden in the clouds. He told every American he met—and who was willing to listen—that he was going to America. His enthusiasm was apparently so infectious that he was even able to persuade an American soldier to teach him to operate his Jeep. Menek could barely reach the clutch when he was finally given the opportunity to drive solo. Even though he was going to a very safe America, he nevertheless was intent on learning to drive, an additional skill that might come in handy in case another war were to break out.

This was also the period when Menek, at thirteen, was going through physical changes. He was experiencing sensations and thoughts that caused him great consternation. These changes both puzzled and concerned him. He instinctively recognized that this was a matter he could not discuss with his mother. She was a "lady," religious, aristocratic, and almost Victorian-like in her habits. There were certain subjects that one never discussed with her. She lived by and adhered to well-established family values and standards that drew strict lines about acceptable behavior and topics of conversation and these lines were never crossed in her presence. Menek intuitively knew this subject would cause him to cross one of those lines.

Neither was he comfortable with the idea of talking to his brother or his newly acquired friends. Menek was embarrassed to confide his worries and feelings. The short stays in various DP camps did not provide enough time to build strong or lasting relationships with friends, at least not relationships in which an adolescent could discuss physical changes that frightened and confused him. Menek needed an adult, a confidant to unload his private thoughts and feelings. He needed someone to tell him that what he was experiencing was a normal, natural process, something his father would have explained gently and tenderly. This was a time when he once again deeply felt the loss of his father, who could have helped him make the transition to physical maturity smoothly and guiltlessly. His father was his hero, his friend and confidant. During this sensitive period, Menek felt his absence more than ever. He searched for the pragmatic old man within him, the inner gyroscope that used to put him straight in difficult times, but here too he kept coming up empty.

This was also a period when Menek developed the conviction that people who had children after the war were selfish and irresponsible—because this world was too cruel to bring children into it. Yet he made himself a solemn promise, that if by some stretch of the imagination in the far-off future he ever did have children, he would do everything in his power to anticipate, prepare and protect them from calamities. He then swore a solemn oath: If he had children, he would do everything humanly and super-humanly possible to make certain that they had their father until the time when they could independently fly from the nest. And if he had a son, things would be different for him.

Chapter Eleven

Journey into the Future

The long awaited letter—with detailed instructions, visas, and passports—finally arrived from America. It contained all the essential documents that might be required along the way. It also contained a cash voucher for minor incidental travel expenses. The HIAS on both sides of the Atlantic also played an important role in facilitating and coordinating aspects of their departure. Various administrators and chaperones made indispensable travel arrangements for the entire contingent of refugees that were slated to make the trip to America. The contingent from Badgastein was to meet up with others along the way to a seaport in Germany from which a ship would ultimately take them across the Atlantic Ocean.

On the day that the travelers set out on their journey, the sun seemed to shine a little brighter, the sky appeared a little bluer, and all the clouds hid respectfully behind the mountains. The heavens trained a strong light on the snowcapped mountains, exposing their breathtaking beauty as they bid farewell to Menek. Even the waterfall sung a rich, voluminous summer aria, which echoed throughout the mountains. These mountains, Mother Nature's wonders, spoke to him. He communicated with them throughout his stay in Badgastein. They were the antidote for the hostile thoughts that he harbored against the whole world. These mountains had allowed him to temporarily become the young thirteen-year-old adolescent that he should have been. Realizing that he was most likely leaving them forever left him with bittersweet feelings.

The first leg of this new journey was Bremerhaven, a German seaport on the North Atlantic more than one thousand kilometers from Badgastein. It was a long leg that they would cover mostly by train. It was a contemplative trip for Menek.

Once again Menek was seated in a train, this time quite comfortably, as it rolled along the German countryside. His eyes scanned the fields, the meadows, and the forests.

He thought it ironic to be traveling once again through Germany. All sorts of emotions welled up within him. Only a year earlier, he and Chamush were trekking from Buchenwald to Wurzen to find their mother. Surely the mood, circumstances, and outlook were significantly brighter this time. Yet Menek was unable to break free from feelings of uncertainty that persistently gnawed at him with all sorts of "What if's. . . ."

While he was in the DP camps, he witnessed a small trickle of survivors arriving from various corners of Europe. Some came out of a variety of hiding places. Others returned from the frozen wastelands of Siberia. The small but constant trickle of arrivals had given him a glimmer of hope that perhaps a loved one would eventually appear. Even now, Menek could not stop his ceaseless speculation that maybe, just maybe, a lost family member would show up. He wondered if they had done everything possible to find missing relatives. If they had not, how could he possibly live with himself if someone showed up years later? Menek worried that the search methodology, hastily established right after the war, may not have been sufficient to ensure that all the survivors would appear on the lists of the living. He was also troubled by the practice of accepting bad news too quickly, reported by those who could have been mistaken.

Menek attempted to share these nagging feelings with his mother on several occasions, but she treated them lightly and dismissed them as transient thoughts that would fade from his mind in due time. Her answers were not enough to relieve the anxiety that persistently hovered over him. And now they were on their way to America, to the other side of the ocean! Menek was tortured by the thought of abandoning lost family members who might still be wandering among the embers of European Jewry.

When they arrived in Bremerhaven, the port of departure, Menek was surprised to see that the number of passengers bound for America had swelled significantly. A warm feeling came over him to see so many survivors like himself preparing to make this pioneering trip. He suddenly felt more secure in the course his mother had set for them. His lingering doubts about leaving Europe eased somewhat as he joined the crowd of prospective voyagers.

Up until this juncture Menek had not given much thought to sailing on an ocean-going vessel. Suddenly he was standing at the pier, gazing at a large American ship used for carrying troops. The name of the ship was the *SS Marine Flasher.* His first thought was, "How can this huge steel structure float in the water?" His momentary hesitation turned in a flash to a desire to board. Menek began to look forward to the adventure of sailing the ocean for the first time.

After seeing the ship, Menek was fully prepared and eager to embrace this new journey. His mother's joy, however, was clearly written all over her face. At the age of forty, after losing her husband, her parents and sisters, she was still able to display considerable excitement at the thought of being reunited with her brothers. Menek was a small child when his uncles left Poland before the war. He did not remember them, but his mother's excitement was sufficiently contagious to inspire him and his brother.

After boarding the ship, the passengers were assigned to their respective compartments and bunk beds. Menek's spirits soared as soon as his feet touched the ship's deck. He had landed in an uncharted world that called for exploration. As soon as they were all settled in and received their orientation, he immediately began to explore every nook and cranny of the ship. His feet carried him from bow to stern and back again. His curiosity was endless. His mother, of course, worried that "God forbid!" he could accidentally fall into the ocean. She generally exercised considerable caution in unfamiliar surroundings, but the young adolescent saw new places as opportunities for exploration. He loved to exercise his new-found freedom. He also felt that he had much to learn in order to catch up to the educational level of boys his age.

His curiosity aboard ship eventually brought him to the entrance of the ship's bridge, but a ship's petty officer made it very clear that entry to the operation center was not included in the price of Menek's ticket. He was sorely disappointed that he could not stand on the ship's bridge to observe the workings of that inner sanctum and get a panoramic view of the whole ocean at the same time. Little did he know that a short ten years later, he would be standing proudly in a U.S. Navy uniform on the bridge of an aircraft carrier, the *U.S.S. Intrepid,* sailing the Atlantic, Mediterranean and Caribbean waters.

The first day out at sea, much to Menek's disappointment, was very foggy. The heavy fog that had rolled in over the English Channel during the night hung over the ship into the following day. It was thick, impenetrable, thus preventing him from seeing the full expanse of the ocean. Menek was out on the deck early the following morning, but he could not even see the faces of passengers from one end of the ship to the other. He had expected to see endless miles of ocean dropping off into the horizon. Instead he heard a continuous melancholy foghorn, blasting an unremittingly warning to potential ships in its path to stay clear. The sad sound of the horn reflected Menek's disillusionment.

But soon Mother Nature cleared away the fog and exposed the Atlantic Ocean in its full splendor. Despite the fact that it was summer, the waters remained choppy and the skies were far from cloudless. Many passengers experienced seasickness during the ocean crossing, but Menek would not allow any physical discomfort to dampen his spirit.

The majesty, the pure grandeur of the ocean did not escape Menek's eyes.

Because he was small he was able to squeeze himself into a small compartment that housed the chain for the anchor. This spot became his "penthouse." It was his own special place from which he could privately look out onto the vast ocean. There he enjoyed a privacy that he rarely experienced in the close quarters of DP life. He spent many quiet hours in his secluded spot, undisturbed by others as he indulged himself in dreams and forever meandering thoughts.

Menek's anticipation grew exponentially with each day that the ship drew closer to the American shore. It seemed to him that most of the passengers on that ship were expecting a family member to greet them. A nervous excitement was evident in every face and every eye. Some people talked without stop, needing to unload their feelings to any stranger willing to listen. Yet others searched out quiet, isolated corners to silently mourn and give vent to their grief.

Menek felt a strong connection to all of them—both the talkers and the reclusive survivors. He was and would forever remain a member of that club. Not just because they were Jewish, but because their similar experiences made it tolerable for them to be together without uttering a single word. This was the glue that held them together: even if they were strangers that had never exchanged a single word before, a common thread held them together. Regardless of their eventual destinations, their common experiences would always unite them. Now these "huddled masses" stood anxiously against the ship's railings, straining to see the beautiful shores of America. Each face had an intense expression, reflecting fervent hopes and fears of starting anew. Menek too pressed hard against the railing, hoping that he would be the first to spot land. He observed all these anxious faces with their eyes fixed on the horizon. They were coming to the "Golden Land." They were coming to start over. To build new lives. To remember and give life to names of loved ones that "were no longer here." To breathe new life into decimated families. To live free and unafraid.

Menek also had a mission. He had promised Jacob the Learned that if he survived, he would tell the world what happened there.

Epilogue

Menek's story is my story—the story of my boyhood in Europe. Upon my arrival in America at the age of thirteen, I began my adult life and took the name "Martin."

The determination to catch up on lost school time became my first priority. I was determined not to allow Hitler to rob me of those vanished years. The three "R's" dominated my initial thrust into the world of education. My brother and I set out in that direction in a Jewish parochial school, a yeshiva. There were several reasons why I agreed to a yeshiva. First, I could not speak English. In a yeshiva I could easily communicate in Yiddish. Second, I was extremely sensitive to religious prejudice. I feared if I were to attend a public school, a careless remark would touch one of my raw nerves and cause me pain that I was not sure I could tolerate anymore. Finally, I felt that if I had to start my schooling at the age of almost fourteen in a significantly lower grade than my peers, Jewish kids and teachers in a yeshiva were likely to treat me more compassionately, particularly if I stumbled a little at the start.

The resolve to learn a *"fach,"* a trade—lest a war broke out again—was so overpowering that after three years I quit the yeshiva and enrolled in a public high school that offered a "trade" curriculum. This move was a disappointing blow to my mother as well as to the principal of the yeshiva, but I could not be dissuaded.

At the same time I was also able to obtain a part-time job, after classes, as a delivery boy. Getting paid for work was a welcome and liberating experience. Even though the pay for my labor was minimal, it nevertheless gave me a much-needed sense of self-worth. It also afforded me the opportunity to purchase mouth-pleasing delicacies that I might not otherwise have been able to afford.

I graduated high school at the age of nineteen and within a few months I enrolled in a two-year electronics technical school, working nights and attending school in the days. Immediately after graduation and receiving my first-class Federal Communications Commission (FCC) license, a highly prized certification, my outlook for the future appeared a little safer. Several months later I was called to serve in the U.S. Military Service, specifically the U.S. Navy. The FCC license plus the electronics education qualified me to be consigned to the Electronics Division.

Serving in the U.S. Navy was a rewarding, enriching, confidence-building experience that I gladly embraced at the time. The sudden awareness that I was now part of the very military organization that liberated me from the chains of hell gave me a great deal of satisfaction. This feeling intensified when I strolled down the streets of European cities in my U.S. Navy uniform. The boost to my morale was immeasurable. It gave me the self-confidence I sorely needed on my return to Europe. Suddenly I was being looked up to, admired and pursued. Only ten years earlier I was looking "up" at the Americans, admiring them and seeking their favor. Now I was on the receiving end of the flattery, even though it made me feel uncomfortable at times.

During my free time on the ship—an aircraft carrier named the *U.S.S. Intrepid*—I seized every opportunity to continue and diversify my education. I enrolled in several correspondence courses. One of my early monthly paychecks went for a down payment on a fifty-volume encyclopedia with the associated "Books of Science" and "Books of Knowledge." Those books in many ways opened up the world to me. I cherished each and every volume throughout my adult life, even when they became worn. Finally and very reluctantly I was forced to lay them to rest in the year 2002, when my computer conspired with the Internet to make them totally archaic. It was a melancholy parting.

After serving two years of active duty in the U.S. Navy, I married a loving, understanding, selfless, compassionate woman who gave me a son and two daughters. We became engaged before I entered the service, but because of my constant fear of possibly "going to war," I insisted on a wedding date after my "safe" return—a concept my American-born fiancée had difficulty understanding at the time. We were married several months after my release from active duty.

A few months after our wedding, I enrolled in a college that offered a night-school curriculum in engineering. After I received a BS in Electrical Engineering, I accepted a position in the field of research and development for nuclear submarines. In the years that followed I continued to diversify my studies in the various engineering sciences, steadily expanding my professional horizon. Eventually, in the early 1970s, I went into private practice, forming my own engineering consulting firm that specialized in air pollution control.

I am considered a "workaholic" by family and friends, partly because I love my work so much and partly because it is so rewarding. I cannot remember a day in the last thirty years that I have not looked forward to going to work. I have been accused by my peers of being a perfectionist and a compulsive. I sometimes think they really do not understand me, and I cannot begin to explain to them my drive to excel. There are so many factors.

In 1994, my son and daughter-in-law awarded me the delicious honor of being called "Zaidy," Grandfather, a title that warms my heart to this very day. There is no other title in this world that could give me a warmer glow. When I look into the eyes of my grandchildren, I have to say "it was all worth it."

Sadly, my mother "is no longer here." Thankfully, we had her with us long enough to celebrate her 90th birthday. She was blessed with the joy of experiencing grandchildren and great-grandchildren. She and I developed a relationship such that verbal communication was often not necessary. In a hall packed with people, our eyes could meet from afar and speak volumes. Her mind and spirit remained sharp until her last day on earth. Only after I became a grandfather myself did I truly understand what she meant when she said of the children, "They are my lifesavers."

My brother became an attorney. After passing the New York State Bar, he went into private practice in New York City. He, too, is a proud Zaidy of grandsons and granddaughters. In America, Henek (Chamush) became Henry Paul. But to me he is, to this very day, Chamush.

We have maintained an unbreakable bond. We frequently get together, often just the two of us. We have made it a practice to visit our mother's grave four times a year. One of those visits is in memory of our father. I have inwardly designated her grave as the marker for all of our family members who lost their lives in the Holocaust. Until her passing, we had no graves or markers to visit. So her *"matzaivah,"* her gravestone, is a gravestone for them all.

Hanue and Motek left Germany and came to America shortly after we did. They raised a family in St Louis and eventually moved to Israel. They, their children, grandchildren and great-grandchildren now live in Jerusalem.

Life in the United States has been absolutely wonderful. My work, which includes lots of travel, both domestic and international, has been very rewarding. But I never fail to experience a warm inner glow whenever I set foot again on American soil after returning from a trip abroad. This country opened its doors to me when I was penniless, dejected and very bitter. It offered me the freedom and opportunity to reach for and achieve a modicum of success and happiness, and so I say without reservation, "Thank you, America!"

I have tried to report, as best as my memory served me, an account of events as I lived them and saw them with my own eyes. These early childhood-robbing events shaped my vision of life, my very nature, and my soul. Scenes from sixty years ago continue relentlessly to invade my sleep. I fervently pray that, after having written this book, I will at long last discover the inner peace that has eluded me for so many years.

This autobiography is the fulfillment of an obligation to the many victims of the Holocaust whose voices were stilled before their time and whose lives—and deaths—should not be forgotten. It is my fervent hope that books like mine will blunt any revisionist attempts to deny the murders of the innocent souls who suffered at the hands of the Nazis. Jacob the Learned's admonition to "tell the world what happened" still echoes in my ears, and I have taken this obligation upon myself as a survivor's mission.

Chamush and Menek (me), in Tarnobrzeg, 1936.

My father, Marcus Schiller. This was his passport photo.

"Bubby," my grandmother, Chaya Zelda Rothwachs.

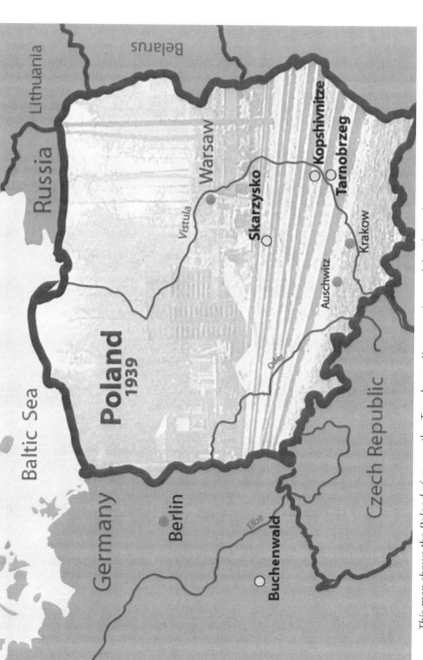

This map shows the Poland of my youth—Tarnobrzeg, Koprzywnica, and the Skarzysko and Buchenwald camps.

KL.: Buchenwald — Jugendlich

Häftl.-Nr.: 68333 P

Häftlings-Personal-Karte

Fam.-Name: SCHILLER
Vorname: Menex
Geb. am: 13.3.32 in: Tarnobrzeg
Stand: led. Kinder: —
Wohnort: W.O., Kr. Jaroslau, Distr. Krakau
Strasse: 11, Mickiewicza 14
Religion: mos. Staatsang.: Pole
Wohnort d. Angehörigen: Mutter
Sara Sch.

Eingewiesen am: 5.8.44
durch: RSHA
in KL.: Buchenwald
Grund: Polit. Pole — Jude
Vorstrafen:

überstellt
an KL.
an KL.
an KL.
an KL.
an KL.
an KL.

Entlassung:
am: durch KL.:
mit Verfügung v.:

Strafen im Lager:
Art: Grund:

Personen-Beschreibung:
Grösse: 127 cm
Gestalt: schlank
Gesicht: oval
Augen: blau
Nase: klein
Mund: gew.
Ohren: gew.
Zähne: vollst.
Haare: dunkelbraun
Sprache: poln., deutsch

Bes. Kennzeichen: keine
Charakt.-Eigenschaften:

Sicherheit b. Einsatz:

Körperliche Verfassung:

Bemerkung:

This document is from the Nazi file on me as a prisoner at Buchenwald.

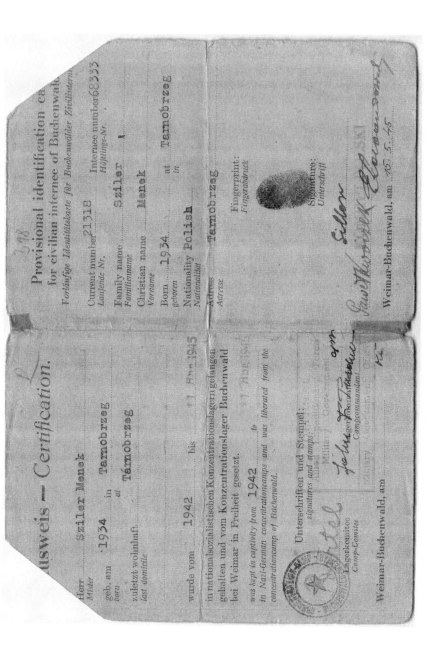

The American Army issued us identification documents upon liberation from Buchenwald.

A reunited family in Wurzen, several months after liberation:
Chamush, my mother, my cousin Hanue, and me.

*We were "Displaced Persons" after the war, wondering where we could go.
Here I am with a friend in Badgastein, 1946.*

*In 1956, I was in the U.S. Navy, cruising the Mediterranean
on the aircraft carrier, the U.S.S. Intrepid.*

I returned to Poland in 2004 at the urging of my son Marc, who wanted to take this "heritage trip." Here we are in Warsaw.

Crossing the Visla River once more—from Tarnobrzeg to Koprzywnica—this time with my son Marc, 2004.

I revisited the site of the Skarzysko labor camp with my son Marc, daughter Susan, wife Elaine (above) and daughter-in-law Karyn (who is taking the picture).

A monument in memory of the Jews who perished in Skarzysko. Elaine and Susan are standing to the left of the monument; Marc is talking to the guides on the right.

The back of the Skarzysko monument bears an inscription in Hebrew.

Buchenwald's main entrance gate still looks forbidding in 2004.

All that remains of "Block #30"–the barrack of the Russian prisoners-of-war–is this concrete marker.

At Buchenwald, 2004: "I survived!"

About the Author

Martin Schiller is an electrical engineer specializing in air pollution control. Born in 1933 in Tarnobrzeg, Poland, he and his immediate family lived in the city of his birth until the outbreak of World War II in 1939. From 1942 to 1945, he was a prisoner in two concentration camps, Skarzysko-Kamienna and Buchenwald. After liberation from Buchenwald, he was shuffled in and out of various DP (Displaced Persons) camps.

He came to the United States in 1946 where he began his formal education. In 1970 he formed his own engineering consulting firm serving a domestic and international clientele. In 1986, he served as a member of a scientific delegation invited by the People's Republic of China for the exchange of industrial air pollution control technology. He lectures to scientists and engineers, and has written on the subject of his research. He also gives talks to high school students about his experiences during the Holocaust.

He lives with his wife Elaine in Fairfield, Connecticut.